Praise for *The Future-Proof Workplace*

"By anticipating the future we thrive in it. Linda and Morag do an outstanding job of helping us see what is coming and then make both organization and personal choices to live and work better. Their ideas are insightful, stories captivating, and recommendations useful."

—**Dave Ulrich**, Rensis Likert Professor of Business, University of Michigan Partner, The RBL Group

"*The Future-Proof Workplace* provides the insights you need to ensure your organization is prepared today for the changes that are already upon us."

—**Margaret M. Keane**, Chief Executive Officer of Synchrony Financial

"Linda and Morag share their clear thinking regarding the future-proof workplace. It's a new day in the work world, and to stay alive and competitive, employers and employees must understand and appreciate the myriad factors affecting the workplace at an alarming rate. Staying abreast of how globalization, demographic shifts, and technological advances impact our world are the keys to success."

—**Dale Mason Cochran**, President, Concourse Ventures, Inc.

"*Future-Proof* is a home run! It challenges us to embrace the most important discussion every leader must have—how to future-proof their organization."

—**Jason Jennings**, *New York Times* and *Wall Street Journal* best-selling author of *Think BIG-Act Small*, *The Reinventors* and *The High-Speed Company*

"The Future-Proof Workplace highlights a subject other management texts avoid—that the nature of work has changed and yet our approach to work, in many cases, has not. This book is packed with stories and practical approaches and solutions to future-proof your organization."

—Jean Elizabeth Lee, Principal,
PwC Human Capital Consulting

"Recent business and technology shifts have created a workplace that is almost unrecognizable from that of two decades ago. And yet many of our approaches to leadership have remained unchanged. Sharkey and Barrett wake us up—crystallizing the changes and giving us new, values-driven tools for powerful, effective leadership."

—Jim Ludema, PhD, cofounder and director
of the Center for Values-Driven Leadership,
Benedictine University

"Linda and Morag have scored a Touchdown! They have challenged each of us to embrace the most important discussion that should be at the forefront of every organization—how to future-proof your organization in the ever-changing landscape of business."

—Jason Carthen, PhD, The Leadership
Linebacker™, "Are You Living Your Destiny?"

"The Future-Proof Workplace provides valuable insights that will help organizations seize opportunities in this rapidly changing landscape, transforming possible vulnerabilities into a competitive advantage."

—Nazneen Razi, Chief Human Resources
Officer, Health Care Services Corp

THE
future-proof
proof
WORKPLACE

THE
future-proof
WORKPLACE

— SIX STRATEGIES —
TO ACCELERATE TALENT DEVELOPMENT,
RESHAPE YOUR CULTURE,
AND SUCCEED WITH PURPOSE

LINDA SHARKEY, PhD • MORAG BARRETT

WILEY

For general information about our other products and services, please contact our Customer Care Department within the United States at (800) 762-2974, outside the United States at (317) 572-3993 or fax (317) 572-4002.

Wiley publishes in a variety of print and electronic formats and by print-on-demand. Some material included with standard print versions of this book may not be included in e-books or in print-on-demand. If this book refers to media such as a CD or DVD that is not included in the version you purchased, you may download this material at http://booksupport.wiley.com. For more information about Wiley products, visit www.wiley.com.

ISBN 9781119287575 (cloth); ISBN 9781119287643 (ePDF);
ISBN 9781119287742 (ePub)

Printed in the United States of America

10 9 8 7 6 5 4 3 2 1

For Tom, whose love and support made my life sing.

—Linda

For James, Matthew, and Christopher. My future.

—Morag

CONTENTS

FOREWORD

The focus of my entire career has been to assist leaders who are successful to be even better. This is not just my career, it's my purpose. I am very humbled and proud to have been named a number one leadership thinker in the world by Thinkers50. It is a great honor to be recognized for the work that I'm so passionate about by such an outstanding organization.

That's why I'm excited about the book you now hold. *The Future-Proof Workplace* puts forward six critical factors that must be addressed for the twenty-first century. These cannot be ignored in these turbulent times. They must be embedded in how you do business every day or you won't survive.

Whitewater rapids are the new normal in business. Many of the lifeboats captained by twentieth-century leaders will capsize. Linda and Morag lay out powerful research and arguments about why we need to embrace these factors now. How we lead and work today is being shaped by massive globalization, seismic demographic shifts, and game-changing technology.

Jobs that used to be the bedrock of the workforce are disappearing. Leaders with self-centered behavior will go the way of dinosaurs. Toxic cultures are being exposed for what they are and no longer tolerated.

I have had the pleasure to meet both Linda and Morag to exchange ideas and things we have learned. Their experience is not only deep but also wide, spanning many industries and public sector organizations.

I've worked with Linda over the years, and we share a common passion for helping shape great leaders. Linda has successfully used the behavioral coaching process outlined in my book, *What Got You Here Won't Get You There*, in a Fortune 100 company, and in many other organizations.

What most impresses me about this book is that Morag and Linda spell out a winning formula for exactly what leaders need to do to thrive now and continue thriving. They share their vast experience working with Fortune 500 organizations and CEOs to prepare for what is happening tomorrow, today.

The real-life stories and examples they share are fascinating and packed with tips to "future forward" your career. Not only are they serious researchers but they have a wealth of experience as hands-on practitioners.

We are on the cusp of major change. Many of the paradigms that held true in the twentieth century no longer apply. The way we shape and design our workplaces, develop talent and leaders, including our people practices, must be retooled for this century. And it must begin now.

This book is a real pay it forward gift to everyone leading organizations today. Whether you are a CEO, senior leader, team leader, aspiring leader, or human resources professional, this book is a must-read for anyone serious about thriving today—and tomorrow.

—Marshall Goldsmith
Coach, Speaker, Author, and Professor of
Management Practice at Dartmouth
Tuck School of Business

CHAPTER 1

Surviving and Thriving in Turbulence

The future depends on what you do today.
—Mahatma Gandhi

Look out! In workplaces across the globe, conventional wisdom is being thrown out the window.

Approaches that were tried and true are being challenged and debunked. Rules that once made sense no longer seem to apply. Everything around us seems to be in flux—from how we conduct ourselves to how companies are functioning.

For example, just 61 companies that were in the Fortune 500 in 1995 were still on the list in 2015. Only 12 percent remained.[1]

Products that were staples are going away forever. Good-bye landline telephones, cable television, and personal computers. The music industry has been changed forever by downloads and streaming. While few use single-tasking cameras, more than 20 million photos are uploaded to social media every minute of every day.

Information ricochets around the world in mere seconds. Facts are checked instantaneously. Truth can be uncovered quickly, and fiction can be spread just as quickly. As a result, politics in most countries are in a constant state of upheaval.

It's a strange new world, and all indicators predict it will only get stranger.

TODAY, NOT TOMORROW

The future of work is not tomorrow. The future of work is today!

In our work with business leaders and teams around the world, we see too many companies missing out—still operating according to twentieth-century mind-sets, practices, and technologies.

We also see the careers of too many gifted individuals needlessly stalled, and ended, because of ignorance or fearful resistance.

It doesn't have to be this way. We want you, your career, and your company to be future-proof. That's why we're sharing our perspectives with you and your teams.

There are plenty of writers who give their predictions for the future, and we enjoy many of those books and articles. But this book deliberately avoids the crystal ball. Instead we offer pragmatic business solutions based on our research and experience. Solutions you can, and should, implement today.

The drivers of change in the workplace are hiding in plain sight. We want to challenge your thinking by exploring six factors, because the way we think about tomorrow influences what we do today.

WAVES OF CHANGE

There are three waves of change that test the limits of human convention and create havoc—and opportunity—in the workplace:

1. Digital technology—the increasing ability to create new ways of doing things.

2. Demographics—the changing mix of, and interaction among, people.

3. Globalization—people's ability to do business in a shrinking world.

These waves of change are having a profound impact on how society, politics, business relationships, and innovation are shaping the twenty-first century. The ways we created strategy, managed people, and built organizations no longer apply.

As a result, power is shifting in ways that make many uncomfortable, others exhilarated, and leave some just shaking their heads wishing for the calmer waters of the "good old days." Of course, change has been wreaking havoc on the status quo since the beginning of mankind. What's new today is the pace of change.

New technology and globalization, in the broadest sense, have always been around. It's the pace and reach of change that are transforming everything we do in business. Think about how the automobile changed not only transportation but how, when, where, and what people purchased.

Can you imagine life today without electric light? This invention revolutionized commerce, manufacturing, and almost every industry.

In their time, just over 100 years ago, these examples were seismic shifts for people. The changes created new business opportunities overnight while destroying other industries. They disrupted whole industries, shifted the skills required for workers, and changed the work environment forever.

And let's be frank, there will be winners and losers, as there always have been as the world spins into the future.

DIGITIZATION AND CHANGE

Last night, while you were sleeping, white collar jobs were being replaced—by computer algorithms.

In the financial sector, software can analyze data, reveal trends, and pose probabilities faster than a human analyst can open a spreadsheet. We are able to mine data for predictions that we could never see previously. This analysis enables us to debunk myths and see new solutions to problems that we could not comprehend before.

These insights will change how we practice medicine, how insurance is sold, and how we transport ourselves to work—or stay home to work.

Today's 3D printers can create almost anything we can imagine. And our cars want to drive themselves! Robots and artificial intelligence are taking over tasks humans once did. In fact, one hotel in Japan is staffed by robots, with only a skeleton crew of humans.

But the new discoveries of the twenty-first century are only just beginning to be realized. A 2014 survey of executives by Forrester/Russell Reynolds cited that over 75 percent of those in the finance, health care, and government sectors believe that their business will be significantly disrupted in the next 12 months.

In the past few years we've seen Netflix go from darling to dumpster—twice! You can bet its executives, and every other media company, is looking to analytics to tailor content by region and by user in order to ride the wave of the future.

A "me too" strategy is not a strategy. If you're copying a business model, you're building in obsolescence and extinction.

Established corporations known as manufacturers, like General Electric, are working to reposition themselves as tech companies. GE is moving its headquarters to Boston, a decision we believe is intended to move the company closer to innovation hubs like MIT.

NV "Tiger" Tyagarajan, president and CEO at Genpact, LLC, recently shared with us that Genpact does not have corporate headquarters and instead spreads its teams around the world in hubs close to their customers. He also noted that their ability to use robots made communication with customers instantaneous.

Through the robot interface, the customer, sitting in New York, could meet the team—based in Poland—that would work for his organization and understand how its processes would be managed. It is quite revolutionary.

CHANGING DEMOGRAPHICS

Much is written today about the millennial generation. And much of it is derisive: "Millennials don't want to work hard. They want to be immediately rewarded with big jobs."

Go back 30 or 40 years and read books and articles about the young people coming into the workforce, and you'll see the same criticisms and concerns. In fact, the same themes were a part of social commentary 1,000 years ago.

Yes, millennials are different, but every new generation has challenged conventional ways of doing things. And there is one constant: the entry-level generation cannot understand why they are not getting the big jobs in three years. And they have much to say about how things should be done.

Millennials have more sophisticated information tools and are usually more adept at using them in the workplace. In other words, most have the data and social skills to back up their assertions.

Children today know more because they can discover information much more quickly—and with the right environment, they can use that information to create exciting products and services. Today's 5-year-olds can create items that a 12-year-old could not create 10 years ago, or adults a generation ago.

There always has been, and always will be, generations that challenge the status quo with more knowledge and creative capability than their predecessors. But the new dynamic is how different generations must coexist in larger numbers in the workplace.

Increased health and longevity has a huge impact on the workforce. For many, retirement at the end of a career no longer makes sense, but sabbaticals during careers may.

In the past, people retired at age 65, expecting a lifespan of about 10 more years. Today, many young people can expect to be active and productive for 20 or 30 years past age 65. The 100-year life will be a reality for many. The trend also means there will be many generations at work. This is the first time in history that five generations are in the workplace together.

GLOBALIZATION IS NOW

The ability of more people to move around with easier access to transportation has created huge upheaval in societies. It is hard today to find a truly homogeneous national culture. Even the traditionally insular country of Japan finds itself needing to embrace immigrants from other parts of the world to fuel its economic growth.

Going back to where everyone is "just like us" is not an option. The old days are gone forever—or rather—the perception of the old days.

Humans are explorers by nature. And we're naturally cautious. Whole societies were set up to ward off onslaughts of others into their tribes. The story here is not just globalization and demographic shifts, but how easy it is for people to move around the world now—whether virtually or in person.

Societies are no longer as homogeneous as they were before, which can create tension in how work is done. This new era of globalization is a business phenomenon that is outpacing societies and outpacing companies.

Talent mobility has increased dramatically and that trend will continue. Once people get the taste of new workplace opportunities, as well as new products and services, they can never go back.

Shock and Awe

Along with change comes disruption. And with disruption comes opportunity. Jobs and companies are going away in the blink of an eye, and start-ups are appearing just as fast. How many cell phones have you had in the past five years? The pace of change is only increasing.

The author Alvin Toffler predicted this in his seminal book, *Future Shock*. The future that Toffler predicted in 1970 is upon us—and has been for many years. He predicted the explosion of information sharing and the disruption of the formalized workplace culture.

Despite the writings of Toffler and other futurists, most people—and most companies—have not stayed ahead of the waves of change.

We have seen through our research, discussions with leaders, best-selling authors, and many of our Fortune 500 clients that the three waves of change are causing the following six factors to emerge. These factors have everything to do with how we deliver goods and services, motivate and engage people, and build relationships to fulfill our shared need for a sense of contribution in our daily lives.

SIX FACTORS OF CHANGE

Here are six factors transforming the workplace from the twentieth to the twenty-first century.

Six Factors	Twentieth Century Attributes	Twenty-First Century Attributes
1. Leadership	Command and control	Flexible, people-focused, shared, values-based
2. Culture	Uniform and not driven into fabric of the organization	Values-driven and embedded into organization decision making and processes
3. Organizing Principles	Mission, vision, shareholder value	Purpose, compelling social impact, customer endearment
4. Relationships	Individualistic, team-focused, and transactional; not concerned with relationships	Interdependent, deliberate, personal, and emotional

| 5. Diversity and Inclusion | Concentrated power, quotas driven, and program-focused | Recognizing unconscious bias and brain science reality of differences— distributed power |
| 6. Technology | Process improvement focus | Innovation-, data-, and fact-based decisions and digital advancement |

These factors require considerable reshaping of fundamentals in any enterprise:

- How you develop people

- How you organize work to deliver value to your customers

- What human relations practices you put into place to advance your workforce

Google, and other forward-thinking companies, have proven that emotional connections are the key to a successful twenty-first-century business. And all six of these factors require a fresh look at the human side of business.

Robots and Artificial Intelligence may demonstrate logic, but they have yet to exhibit heart and emotion (unless you are the Tin Man from *The Wizard of Oz*). They aren't able to display the truly unique aspects of humanness.

We may be in the midst of a digital revolution, but it's the *people* revolution that will determine whether we ride the waves of change or drown.

Let's look at these six factors in a bit more detail.

1. Leadership

More has been written about leadership than probably any other business topic. Search for "leadership books" on Amazon and you'll get to sort through almost 200,000 results.

Still, for some reason, we often get it wrong.

We've seen management in the financial sector ignore technology, choosing to resist computerization with the excuse of not wanting to disrupt their employees. As a result, entire departments, and companies, were wiped out.

In the end, company success boils down to leaders: what they value and how they behave.

While much was espoused about empathic leadership, the twentieth-century leadership style was, and still is, predominantly "command and control." According to Harry Kraemer, former CEO of Baxter, and professor at Northwestern University's Kellogg School of Management, only about 20 percent of leaders practice inclusive, people-focused, and values-driven leadership.

Command and control is the default position of leaders when under intense deadlines and profit pressure. While leaders may wish to adopt a different posture, the culture invariably drives them to conform to "the way things are done around here."

We've worked with many executives to help them change their leadership style, but when new ideas are introduced, the cultural "antibodies" drive out the change agents. The inertia is caused by other leaders in the business who don't walk the talk, and everyone knows it except them!

In the previous century, leadership referred to the C-Suite. But business leadership exists in every department and inside every person.

The twenty-first century demands a shift in leadership to be one of engagement, collaboration, and adaptability. These are also the hallmarks of organizations that can innovate.

Without leaders who can appreciate other points of view and engage with others in an authentic way, organizations will not survive. Globalization, demographic shifts, and technological advances are here to stay. Leaders today must not only accept this fact but embrace it. They must be transparent, because others will find them out—and quickly.

Leadership is the critical factor. Without a shift in our leadership mind-set and our leadership behavior, none of the following factors will be future-proofed.

2. Culture

In the late twentieth-century, the notion of corporate culture was beginning to get some traction. Leaders realized they could have the best strategy on earth, but if the organizational culture did not embrace the strategy, it was going nowhere. Strained relationships and lack of trust could effectively erode any efforts for strategic implementation, let alone innovation.

We remember talking to leaders many years ago about trust, respect, and other factors that affect culture. Very few "got it." The prevailing view was this is "fluff" and like other soft skills, it didn't matter because it didn't contribute to the bottom line. Most leaders we spoke with said, "We don't have time for this. We are focused on shareholder value."

When there was a deeper understanding of company culture, it focused around uniformity, respectability, and conformity. People were supposed to look and act the same, to give customers a sense of comfort and predictability.

The twentieth-century IBM model comes to mind, with the company-mandated blue suits and briefcases.

The concept of company culture was only understood in the more sophisticated companies, and, in some cases, culture's impact on the bottom line was measured. In fact, a recent *Harvard Business Review* article showed that certain positive cultures could increase productivity.[2]

In the twenty-first century most organizations understand that culture and values have everything to do with profitability. As Peter Drucker once said, "culture eats strategy for lunch."

Leaders now realize that values are the underpinnings of their culture. If they want a culture that truly empowers people, they must behave consistently with those values.

Companies like LinkedIn start their business meetings with a discussion of the culture and how they are living up to those ideals. Decisions about what companies to partner with include serious consideration about compatible cultures. Even at the bottom-line-focused *Wall Street Journal*, you'll often see references to corporate culture as the driving force in success . . . and failure.

A healthy culture, and living the values in daily behaviors, is essential for growth, adaptability, and innovation. No one can be left behind in the creativity department.

3. Organizing Principles

In the twentieth century, almost every medium to large organization had to have a mission and vision. In addition, these organizing principles of mission, vision, and strategy sometimes had values tacked onto the framework.

You'd read the same verbiage on the walls: "We are collabo-rative," said the poster, which was written and posted by the CEO without input from other employees. "We're customer-centric," read the banner, in plain sight of everyone in the long line waiting to speak to a customer service representative.

Companies spent millions developing clever statements, which were highly polished and completely ignored in day-to-day operations.

Everyone knew the real focus was profit and shareholder value. These mission-vision tools did not make a measurable difference in the workplace no matter how hard we consultants tried.

Today, in the twenty-first century, a compelling and impactful purpose, around which teams can get excited, is key. We know from studying the brain that people need an emotional connection to what they do. They need to feel inspired and believe they're making a difference if they are to make a real contribution. It's not enough to keep making a better widget or take more cost out of a process. People want to contribute to the greater good and have pride in what they do, whether they are keeping an airport bathroom clean or figuring out how to provide clean water for everyone on the planet.

Members of the younger generation assess a company based upon their view of the real purpose of the enterprise and how well it is living up to that purpose.

And today, with access to the Internet and the wealth of information at our fingertips, everyone can make an informed decision in about five minutes.

4. Relationships

Historically, many organizations played down the role of personal relationships at work. Work was a place where you did your job and got paid in return. Relationships and social connections happened outside of the office.

If relationships were encouraged, it was in the name of teamwork. But we all know from personal experience that many teams don't work well and are often painful to be a part of.

Efforts at team-building training, Robert's Rules of Order, and using facilitators all got put into play to help people relate better to each other. In some cases it worked and in some it did not. Engagement experts discovered that having good relationships at work was directly correlated to employee retention, but it was still not understood as a key component of successful work environments.

Today a greater understanding of the role of relationships, not only at work but in business is general, is coming to light. Google began an interesting study in 2012 to examine its high-performing teams and determine exactly what made them great.[3]

As it turned out, results had nothing to do with the processes that were put in place to keep teams on track and everything to do with the emotional connection between team members. As humans, we are hardwired for connection, and especially for emotional connection.

This emotional connection made all the difference in what appeared, in some cases, to be a very messy team process.

Reid Hoffman, former chairman of LinkedIn, in his book, *The Alliance*, points out that building alliances and mutual relationships with one's employees is essential. This is the secret glue that keeps people engaged and emotionally connected to the work while they are there. The added benefit is that if an employee leaves, which is happening much more frequently than in the past, they leave as a friend.

5. Diversity and Inclusion

Let's be frank. Diversity has been the focus of many organizations in the latter part of the twentieth century largely because of government mandates and laws—not necessarily because we value differences.

Linda's early career was with Alcoa, a government contractor that had to report how many minority and female employees it employed to meet a quota.

Meeting quotas to ensure diversity seemed to be the prevailing approach adopted by many companies at that time and even now. They did indeed meet the quota, but the diversity was always at the lower levels of the organization and seemed to remain there.

With all the policies, programs, and quotas put in place, the needle has only moved about 17 percent for women in executive positions. An even smaller number are CEOs and a similarly small number for other minorities.

Annual meetings of many organizations are still predominately white and male. Despite the growing availability of paternity leave policies for men, many men are hesitant to take advantage of them. More than half the men surveyed in a recent Deloitte survey said taking the leave would signal a lack of commitment to work, and more than a third said it would jeopardize their jobs.

So much for great policies that don't work because of the inherent bias that exists in organizations and in each individual.

We have to understand the root causes for why the needle has not moved substantially—why women are still earning less than men, and why minorities are still underrepresented.

Based on our research and experience, the root cause is unconscious bias. And by the way, we all have bias. The brain is wired to take mental shortcuts and reacts quickly to the 11,000 cues we receive per minute. In fact, studies of the brain indicate that we do unconsciously gravitate to people of our own "tribe."

Our mind and emotions react before we're even aware of it. Is it any wonder organizational change is so challenging?

In order to create a truly inclusive environment with a level playing field for all, we need to understand the role of unconscious bias and the role the brain plays in our ability to connect with people who are different from us.

It is heartening to hear the dialogue going in this direction at some of the leading corporations. And the good news is, according to leading neuroscience researchers, the brain can be consciously rewired.

6. Technology

In the twentieth century, computing technology was in its infancy. It was used to speed communication, make information more readily accessible, and improve work processes.

Tech was hardware-driven and infrastructure-focused. Efficiency was the primary goal, and sometimes the only goal.

The twenty-first-century breakthrough in technology was largely missed: the ability to communicate, collaborate, and enjoy our work. But it's not too late. We'll address this and the other factors in future chapters.

The twenty-first-century breakthrough in IT is about discovering patterns that were previously invisible. For example, predicting certain outcomes, particularly in medicine, will forever change health care and health care systems.

Because of these trends, the organizational basics need reinvention, re-tooling, and in some cases rejection, never to see the light of day again.

LOOKING AHEAD

How we manage and develop people will have to be dramatically rethought. Standard classroom training will no longer be the norm. With the rapid pace of change, people will need to learn improvisation to build on each other's ideas. Learning must take place in real time.

Empathy must be emphasized by encouraging employees to consider the experiences of others. Ford Motor Company has design engineers wear weighted "empathy bellies" to attempt to simulate the experience of being pregnant.

Learning will be relationship driven, as it is at Menlo Innovations, which pairs people up for short projects and then moves them around to work with others—learning and building relationships at the same time.

Office configurations of the twentieth century and standardized cubicles will be a thing of the past. Spaces are being designed for creativity and comfort as at Saudi Aramco's new offices. Aramco is the world's largest oil company, and they redesigned its standard boxy buildings for a network of honeycomb cells. These cells have no doors that act as a barrier to collaboration, and are decorated in bright colors, with soft furnishings that encourage people to sit, talk, and innovate. The twenty-first-century workspaces will be about ideas, creativity, and collaboration. And in many cases we won't need office space at all.

Human Resources policies need to be examined for inherent bias and relevance in this digital age.

Your career will change. And that can be a good thing. What will never change is the need for personal connection and interaction.

The twenty-first century is going to be messy, and it will require more agile approaches to work. Change is not new. It has happened before throughout our history and will continue in the future, far beyond our lifetimes. However, today, the impact is fast and profound. We are being challenged, as humans, to rethink and redefine our role in the world, and especially at work. In fact the digital revolution is challenging us to consider the ultimate question—what does it mean to be human?

THE FUTURE HAPPENED YESTERDAY

> The future is already here—
> it's just not evenly distributed.
> —William Gibson, *The Economist*

Can you survive all this change? Of course you can, but you must prepare and act now!

The energy sector will grow, but coal mines are not coming back. That canary died decades ago. Admit it. And admit the change you face in your industry.

In the following chapters we'll cover each of the transformational factors that are here now and provide real-life examples and recommendations to future-proof your company—and career.

These times, if embraced with purpose, can make a difference in your workplace and create a company where everyone matters. The future isn't for the chosen few but for those who care enough to help others transform their lives.

Buckle your seat belt, if we still have seat belts in self-driving cars, and get ready for the ride of your lifetime. For those who can stomach it, the future is bright for your company, your career, and your colleagues.

CHAPTER 2

Leadership

Leading the Future

I slept and I dreamed that life is all joy. I woke and I saw that life is all service. I served and saw that service is a joy.

—Khalil Gibran

We walked into the executive meeting after preparing for days with our team to deliver the much-anticipated proposal.

Our team had worked hard to capture what the executives wanted. Many long days and nights were consumed with getting just the right tone, providing the facts, and offering some cutting-edge solutions.

As we waited outside the conference room, we heard arguing and yelling inside the room. We all looked at each other with concern. We'd heard that the executive team did not get along and its members were always trying to outdo each other. Each one wanted to be the smartest person in the room and often showed it by pointing out small flaws that had little impact on the proposal.

Colleagues often came out of those meetings discouraged and demoralized. It appeared that was going to happen again with our team.

As the doors opened, a colleague walked out of the room and said, "Good luck. They are really in rare form today." This team was sent back to the drawing board again because the executive team members were grandstanding and could not agree.

We knew their pain. We had experienced it before. They had already spent many long hours on their proposal, and they would now have to spend many more. All the team wanted at this point was to get a plan approved so they could move forward. They just wanted to get on with it.

It was our turn at bat, and the same result, or nonresult, happened. We were sent back to the drawing board with a completely new direction. As we left the room, we overheard one executive say, "I found the one error in that proposal."

As we walked down the hall to face another round of pitch-making, one of our team members said, "I wish they would just agree on what they wanted, or just tell us what to do. This guessing game is exhausting."

AN OLD BRAND OF LEADERSHIP

What was surprising is that this group of executive leaders had no idea about the reputation they were creating. Word spread regularly about how dysfunctional the executives were and how poorly they treated those that worked for them. Not all of the executives acted badly, but enough did that the whole group got tainted. No one wanted to make presentations to them, and everyone in the organization was clued in to their behavior.

These executives thought they were providing brilliant guidance and simply being tough when they did not get what they wanted. The truth was they were oblivious to the needs of anyone else. Staff used to call meeting with the executive team the "proctologists meeting," and when one particularly vile female executive left, internal e-mails rang out with "Ding dong, the witch is dead."

Soon, the tough culture was entrenched, and the company was going downhill.

These are leaders who see staff members as being there to make them look good. Their days are consumed with making sure they get the accolades and the next promotion. They come down hard on those who work for them if they make innocent mistakes, try new things, or just plain don't agree with them.

These are the command and control leaders of the past. Command and control leaders truly believe they have all the answers.

This style has been honed over the centuries through feudal systems, royal dominance, and bureaucratic organizations. It may well be unconscious behavior on the part of many leaders, which is why it is so hard to change.

Self-Focused Leadership

Some command and control leaders can be nice and treat people well but still make it clear they will have their way. They're not interested in new ideas or approaches. They are the benevolent dictators.

In the early twentieth century, this leadership style was alive and well. People came to work and did what they were told. When William Harley offered a new approach to a supervisor at the company he was working for, his boss literally smashed the invention and told him to get back to work.

What did Harley do? He continued his innovative project outside of his workplace, and the iconic brand was eventually born: Harley-Davidson motorcycles.

Even though this dysfunctional management style was popular in the early industrial era, and for that matter through the centuries, it did not ultimately thwart human creativity. It just made it harder to bring innovation to the workplace.

Studies of the brain show that humans are creative by nature and when put in situations where they can be creative their brains actually light up. But we also know that when messages have been sent over the centuries that command and control is good and empowering others shows weakness, our brains have been unconsciously programmed to model that leadership style.

GREED

You don't have to read many business headlines to see greed in action.

Volkswagen cut corners on fuel emissions equipment and cheated on the tests and only confessed when caught. Mylan became a household word by upping the price of a life-saving medication. The CEO defended the action because of a need to make more profit, and gave herself a hefty raise as a result. It only became an issue when there was a huge public outcry.

Wells Fargo encouraged staff, 5,300 to be exact, to use customer data to create millions of bogus credit card accounts and move money to those accounts through a cross-selling program. Elizabeth Warren at a Senate hearing had this to say about the CEO of Wells Fargo: "And when it all blew up, you kept your job, you kept your multi-multimillion-dollar bonuses, and you went on television to blame thousands of $12-an-hour employees who were just trying to meet cross-sell quotas that made you rich."

Not only are some of these acts unethical, they are illegal. They are fueled by personal greed, at the expense of those they lead.

It is this culture of greed that puts average, honest workers under stress to deliver results at all costs. In order to get compliance, leaders resort to command and control, and followers comply.

We've seen numerous examples in our work with leaders across the globe. While working with a Wall Street brokerage firm, we had the opportunity to talk to executives about a leadership development program we were creating for them. Three of the top leaders informed us that all they really cared about was profit. We were astonished at their blunt honesty, though, sadly, unsurprised by the leadership mantra being exhibited.

It later became apparent that the top leaders structured deals solely to avoid taxes and borrowed money from the company treasury for personal projects (signing promissory notes but not paying back the initial loans), which made them large sums of money.

They created a culture of *make money at all costs*, and it was pervasive throughout the company. A broker actually told us he could do anything he wanted and we could not stop him because he made too much money to be fired.

The leadership development program we designed for this company was a real eye opener to the participants. It's ironic that the program was designed to help leaders be more collaborative and to combat the poor employee engagement scores the firm consistently received. We taught leaders about the true nature of leadership, and they contrasted it to what they were experiencing every day. Many of the leaders in our training program resigned for greener pastures and better leadership values.

This firm no longer exists. It was bought out by another organization in a fire sale. The executives walked out with bundles of money after the sale, and many mid-level professionals were laid off.

THE CONSEQUENCES

Today with social media word gets out quickly about where to work and who to work for.

The emphasis on leadership over the past 30 years has grown intense. Organizations are trying to change the model to focus on empowerment and self-actualized achievement rather than control.

Jim Kouzes, author of *The Leadership Challenge*, cited a study he carried out in a recent conversation. He asked a group of leaders to rate themselves as leaders on a number of dimensions. They all gave themselves above-average marks.

Jim then asked their subordinates to rate them, and the marks were significantly lower. Leaders are still out of touch with how they are viewed and how well they are actually doing.

Command/control and greed often go hand in hand and aren't sustainable in a future-proof world of today and tomorrow. People are more educated, more quickly connected, and unhealthy social constraints are breaking down. People are no longer as afraid of speaking up and losing their jobs. Retirement savings are portable. Health care is more accessible. The "brilliant jerk" can no longer be tolerated.

The rules of the workplace are changing quickly. Expectations of new entrants are different. Today's workforce is not asking to be engaged, it expects to be engaged.

TWENTY-FIRST-CENTURY LEADERSHIP

Of course, history and business are also full of examples of great leaders. But the nexus of command/control and greed worked in the past—producing obedience and productivity, albeit temporarily.

Because of this, great leadership has been rare. And the perennial debate has been whether great leaders are born or made.

Leadership of the future is really the same kind of leadership that's always been effective.

Cultural pressures and greed are like magnets, constantly trying to pull leaders off track. And today, there are new pressures and new changes. Staying on track is not only important—it is essential for survival.

Let's be honest. We know what good leadership is, but we often don't model it. Why? The purpose and measure of business has been too frequently identified solely as profit.

The twenty-first-century leader understands that business is also about values, purpose, and solving problems. We all have an opportunity to encourage leadership to blossom and become the norm.

Good leaders have a good purpose and are clear about their values.

THE PRIVILEGE OF LEADERSHIP

Leadership is a privilege. It is not bestowed on a certain few who are deemed wiser or by the luck of some draw. Some of the great leaders over the centuries have left lasting legacies and, in some cases, did not hold formal leadership positions. Great leaders lead wherever they are and whatever their career level.

If you ever watch the television show *Undercover Boss*, you see how out of touch many leaders can be from the day-to-day operation. But in these situations leaders are trying to learn what really goes on. They are not trying to catch someone doing something wrong; they are trying to catch people doing things right and reward them!

When they see obstacles in the way of good people trying to do the right thing, they remove the obstacles. They learn a lot from the experience and also understand how tough some of these jobs are. They build relationships that last.

Leaders who see their role as a privilege understand that they have a responsibility to the people who depend on the organization for their livelihood, their families, and communities.

What does it mean to have the privilege of leadership? As a leader you have a great responsibility—not to yourself—but to those you lead. You cannot trash a company like Enron did and not expect serious repercussions.

PERSONAL VALUES CREATE COMPANY VALUES

Leaders need to be clear on their personal values first before adopting and modeling company values. Values must be internalized.

Here's a personal story from Linda, from when she was in graduate school. A professor asked what her values were. She froze and felt a knot in her stomach. She honestly had no idea.

How many of you would have a similar response? Ever felt like a deer in headlights? In our work with leaders around the globe we will often ask this question as part of our leadership programs.

The component part of being a leader isn't platitudes but coming to grips with values on a personal level. Before you select inspirational-sounding phrases for your company or department, be solid on your own personal values.

Joshua Chamberlain, a Civil War colonel in the Union army, was faced with a pivotal leadership challenge. One hundred twenty troops had attempted desertion and were arrested. The typical punishment for this crime was to be shot by firing squad.

But he and his troops faced a daunting battle the next day. Colonel Chamberlain had a monumental decision to make. He gathered the deserters and addressed them. Here are some excerpts from that speech:

> I've been ordered to take you men with me, I'm told that if you don't come I can shoot you. Well, you know I won't do that. Maybe somebody else will, but I won't, so that's that. Here's the situation, the whole Reb army is up that road a ways waiting for us, so this is no time for an argument like this, and I tell you. We could surely use you fellas, we're now well below half strength . . .
>
> You know who we are and what we are doing here, but if you are going to fight alongside us, there are a few things I want you to know. This regiment was formed

last summer in Maine. There were a thousand of us then, there are less than 300 of us now.

All of us volunteered to fight for the Union, just as you have.

Some came mainly because we were bored at home, thought this looked like it might be fun. Some came because we were ashamed not to. Many of came because it was the right thing to do. And all of us have seen men die.

This is a different kind of army. If you look back through history, you will see men fighting for pay, for women, for some other kind of loot. . . . We are an army out to set other men free. America should be free ground, all of it, not divided by a line between slave states and free—all the way from here to the Pacific Ocean.

Here we judge you by what you do, not by who your father was. . . . It's the idea that we all have value—you and me. What we are fighting for, in the end, we're fighting for each other. Sorry, I didn't mean to preach. You go ahead and you talk for a while. If you choose to join us and you want your muskets back, you can have them. Nothing more will be said by anyone anywhere.

If you choose not to join us, well then you can come along under guard, and when this is all over, I will do what I can to ensure you get a fair trial, but for now we're moving out.

"Gentlemen, I think if we lose this fight we lose the war, so if you choose to join us, I will be personally very grateful."

Amazingly, all but six of the deserters immediately rejoined the regiment, and another four joined shortly after. They went on to win the battle of Little Round Top, which proved to be a pivotal victory.[1]

Notice how this leader operated according to his values in the face of literal life and death decisions. Kind of makes the next staff meeting seem a bit more manageable, doesn't it?

Life and business throw tests our way. Without values you won't be an effective leader.

Solid personal values give you the platform and the confidence to translate those convictions into authentic company values.

Authentic values create a vibrant company culture. Values are the DNA of culture.

This is where the DNA culture is born and grows.

No matter where you are on the organizational chart, begin applying and articulating your values.

DEFINING VALUES

Value is no longer defined by how much money a company makes but rather moving toward how much good it contributes to society.

There is a moral fiber in the new leaders of today. They do not start their discussions with financial charts but rather with how the company is living its values. Leaders who understand that it is a privilege to lead others have a very strong moral compass. They lack the hubris of the past and the trappings of the role.

When leading a session for a company's 140 global leaders, we discussed their values. They shared honestly about how well they lived their values at work. In some cases they were ashamed of what they did and didn't do.

The senior team did not blame them or punish them for telling the truth. They provided the space and time for their direct reports to discuss what they needed to change. Together they created peer-coaching groups to help support each other in learning how to engage with others.

The CEO did not redirect the conversation to financial outcomes because he knew that without this reflection the financial gains would be short lived.

We love the story Marshall Goldsmith tells about Alan Mulally, former CEO of Ford Motor Co. Mulally started every staff meeting by asking who needed help with what they were trying to do.

In most organizations people would be afraid to admit they needed help. But not on Mulally's team. And the results were astounding. Real teamwork is not fake teamwork. Real teamwork has trust and camaraderie that runs deep and can be seen by all. For Mulally and Ford the message was, *we are all in this together*. What is also interesting is that Ford did not take any of the bailout money during the recent Great Recession and maintained a strong financial presence in the market.

This is leadership that understands it is a privilege to lead. Good leadership drives out fear, builds support for team members, and fosters relational connections.

LEADERS WITH HEART

William Ewart Gladstone, four-time British prime minister during the nineteenth century, famously said, "We look forward to a time when the power of love will replace the love of power. Then will our world know the blessing of peace." Jimi Hendrix sang a similar message in the twentieth century.

In Linda's previous book, *Winning with Transglobal Leadership*, she and her coauthors Nazneen Razi, Peter Barge, and Rob Cooke set out to discover what exactly made great global leaders. They wanted to scientifically discover the key attributes of leaders that were directly correlated to positive business outcomes.

They defined positive business outcomes as: a provable great culture, high employee engagement scores, solid financial results, sustainable performance, and stellar marketplace reputation. They wanted to know what really drove results.

They found five critical dimensions that set these leaders apart from everyone else.

1. They are purpose driven even in times of great ambiguity.

    These are leaders that don't require a mountain of details. They can make sense out of the "trees" and create a compelling purpose for the future. They are purpose driven themselves. They have reflected on who they are and make it a habit. They act with a strong sense of personal purpose about what they are trying to achieve. These people make sense out of chaos and help others see a compelling path forward.

2. They act with heart and love toward those they lead.

    They do not expect others to cater to them. They take a deep interest in their teams and fellow employees. They see their role as helping others be the best they can be. They are personally engaged in the development of others. It is their mission and passion to help others meet their aspirations. They are not the benevolent dictator of the past, rather they create paths and opportunities for people to grow and achieve what they want to achieve professionally.

It was a pleasure to meet with Suhail Bin Tarraf, CEO of Tanfeeth, a United Arab Emirates outsourcing company, and to tour his facility in Dubai. Here is a man who embodies heart. You walk into his facility and everyone knows him, and, as important, he knows his employees. He stops to chat and engages in real conversation with everyone he encounters.

Every day Tanfeeth managers start the morning with a discussion of how their team members are feeling. If someone feels sad or is having a problem at home, they can talk about it. The team rallies around the person to provide support. If the person needs to go home to take care of a sick child or parent, for example, they can leave.

People are grateful for the chance to take care of an issue that is sapping their focus. They come back more determined than ever to do a good job. The remarkable thing about Bin Tarraf is that he would never dream of interrupting one of these meetings for a concern he had, no matter what it was. Allowing people to think through the day and express personal concerns is so important to him that he waits. How many of us can say that?

3. They are team builders but not in the traditional sense.
These leaders are not just about developing their own teams but developing a team spirit in everyone. They create and connect pods of people around the world to solve tough problems. They are boundary-less in how they develop teams. It is about getting the right people

together to tackle issues no matter where they are in the organization, or who they report to.

Organization charts do not bind them, and they don't operate in silos. They don't keep the people who report to them in a box. They willingly get them involved in important purpose-driven projects. When the project is over, team members move on to the next key project.

Rich Sheridan of Menlo Innovations comes to mind when we think about a leader who lives this dimension. He has very few managers in his organization. People either work in pairs or teams to solve customer problems and learn from each other. When the problem is solved, they move on to the next group or team that needs their help or that they need to learn from. Not only is this a great development tool but it also builds strong relationships across the company.

People naturally learn to support and help each other without the constraints of an organization chart and leadership hierarchy.

4. They are highly perceptive.

These are leaders that pick up cues from others and know when others don't understand, or agree. These leaders don't just assume everyone is on board. They spend time understanding the other person's point of view.

A great example of this is Mathew Yu, a team leader from Proctor & Gamble. His job was to go around the world and help bring Lean Six Sigma to all the P&G sites. At first he would give instructions about how to implement Lean Six Sigma. But it was not sticking. People did not follow through. Initially, Yu thought it was because people in the rest of the world were resistant to anything western (ironic given that Six Sigma is based on Kaizen philosophy, which came out of Japan). What he discovered, because he was perceptive enough to see that something else was going on, was that it was not resistance at all. People were anxious to learn, they just did not understand it in their own context.

Yu started with a small "SWAT team" and met with the local teams to explain what they were trying to achieve. They then asked, "How is this done here?"

This one question made all the difference. Teams worked through how they would achieve the goals and outcomes in their country, and embraced the tools. They wanted to learn but just didn't understand how it would work where they were. Yu was so successful that he received many promotions and his process was adopted around the world.

5. Leaders are crystal clear about their values.

They live their values every day but do not impose their values on others. They will never do anything unethical. They have a very strong moral compass. But they understand that they may have to adjust their values slightly to reflect other social and cultural conditions relative to where they are at the time.

Jackie Mitchell Wynn, an executive at Dell EMC, told a story about her son's training at West Point. The teacher posed a question to the class about a meeting that was to take place in Saudi Arabia.

It was a highly sensitive meeting and a very serious situation for our country. The best person to conduct the meeting would be a particular senior officer who is a woman. "You value women's equal rights. What would you do?"

The class had a long debate. Ultimately it was decided that they would not send the women, and they would adjust their values for this situation. They understood that if a woman led the discussion in this environment every Saudi man would walk out of the room, and they would not get to square one.

This scenario is hard to believe, but sometimes you have to adjust your values for the greater good of what you are trying to achieve for others.

In fairness to the Saudis, we have personally seen change in their attitudes toward women. Conversations about women's rights in the workplace and beyond are starting to occur.

These dimensions are the ones that will carry you into the twenty-first century.

A Decision to Lead

Walter McFarland, of Windmill Human Performance, noticed that the greatest leaders had three things in common. "The first big theme was passion," he told us.

"When you read the statements of the people who accomplished the most, it didn't happen by chance. They didn't achieve because they were obsessive or compulsive. They did it because they cared about it, right down to their very DNA."

The second theme: "They seemed consistently able to attach whatever their task was to that higher purpose," Walter said. "It was about changing something in a bigger and better way. It was about the opportunity for people to engage and make a real difference in the makeup of their organizations.

"And the third piece was always that somehow, in the midst of doing these global, galactic, big things, they found time to develop people. They did that without exception."

We couldn't agree more.

"The best way to predict the future is to create it." —Author unknown. (Probably because he or she was busy creating, leading, and empowering others!)

When you practice these three behaviors, not only will you help others and show you care, you will feel great about yourself. You can look yourself in the mirror and say, *I lived my life's purpose. I helped others live their dreams and achieve their goals, no matter who they are, where they live, and what religion they practice.*

This is the power, privilege, and purpose of leadership.

Future-Proof Your Company

- If leading with clear convictions were easy, everyone would do it. Here are some ways to begin. Ask yourself: What guides you in your daily life, and where did you learn those ideals?

- What nonnegotiables will guide you in life and work?

- Ask yourself these questions:

  1. How would others describe me as a leader?

  2. What is driving me to be a leader?

  3. What is the legacy I want to leave?

Reflect on your answers. Share them with trusted colleagues, and write their observations in a journal and see if you like the picture they paint.

FUTURE-PROOF YOUR CAREER

- Pick one behavior that you want to do more of, or less of, to be the leader you want to be. Think about what you are going to do to live that behavior. Start every day this way.

- At the end of the day, note how well you did and when you could have done better. When you have made that behavior a habit, move on to the next. Make this practice part of your lifelong learning process.

CHAPTER 3

Culture

The Key for Innovation and Speed

Marketing promotions may win quarters, but innovation wins decades.

—Former Procter & Gamble CEO Bob McDonald

O ur customers are important to us. Please stay on the line for the next available representative."

The irony of this message sinks in after the first five minutes on hold. During the next five minutes, it becomes clear the values of the organization are aligned around cost savings—with the naive hope you'll ignore their actions and believe their words.

Thankfully, there are organizations that are a delight to do business with, where employees go out of their way to help you— and help each other. This atmosphere makes you want to jump for joy and figure out how to clone the whole experience.

WHAT'S THE DIFFERENCE?

The difference in these scenarios is culture. And cultural innovation should be a top priority for your company.

We have seen, and you've probably experienced, workplaces where managers yelled at their teams. People keep their heads down to avoid doing something wrong and, as a result, avoid doing something right. The culture of these places tamps down good ideas instead of bringing out the best in people.

What about your organization? Have you ever had someone tell you your idea wasn't good and then share it as his or her own? Or say he wants creativity and innovation only to criticize every new perspective?

Good ideas are regularly squashed never to see the light of day. You get the sense your boss really does not want good ideas that don't originate from him. So, as the employee, you stop and you do as you are told. You know the written rules of the company really are not true and that your place is to be quiet, follow orders, and survive if you can.

Here are real examples from leaders and organizations we have worked with that depict the situation mentioned above.

While we were coaching a senior leader, he vented that his staff lacked creativity. He said, "they never have any good ideas when I ask for them. They just look at me blankly. It's so frustrating."

When we interviewed his team the picture became clearer. He sent the message to his employees that he really didn't want new ideas from them. He only wanted his own ideas. They shared how they wasted lots of time and energy in coming up with new ideas just to see them go nowhere.

When the team feedback was shared with the leader he was shocked and did not believe it. He actually thought he had a lazy and uninspired staff. The staff definitely was not lazy or uninspired, just extremely frustrated. The boss was creating a culture of low accountability and complacency and did not even know it.

We were told about how a leader in another global organization would grade the work submitted by his team. Work was returned with "red lines and comments," and ideas that were deemed particularly lacking were often displayed on what was known as "the wall of shame." Even years after it was dismantled, the wall still cast a long shadow. New ideas were shared cautiously, if at all.

Contrast this with the leadership style of Suhail Bin Tarraf, who we discussed in the previous chapter. He had a "wall of fame" to encourage great customer service ideas and celebrate his team.

These examples amplify how critically important culture is to any organization, especially one that needs fresh ideas and speed to succeed—which is every industry and every organization today.

You will either get the culture you deserve, or the culture you want. Don't leave it to chance, pay attention, take action, and make sure that it is the latter!

We recently spoke with Inc. president and editor-in-chief, Eric Schurenberg, who said, "It's a difficult thing to adapt to a world in which technology and the expectations of customers are just constantly in flux. Business cultures that are more adaptive, that are more horizontal, where leaders treat their employees as the source of ideas and the source of creativity are going to be able to adapt the most. There will be a true competitive advantage for companies that treat their most important assets as real assets."

CULTURE AND THE CUSTOMER

Traditional organizations, spawned in the industrial era, had innovation locked up with their research scientists in their labs. These organizations believed their mainstream employees were there to carry out orders, not to think. Traditional organizations of the twentieth century operated with controls and principles that viewed the workforce as the arm that got the work done, not the brain.

An interesting shift happened over time. Customers started expecting better service and had more choices about where they could spend their money.

Along comes Amazon. Amazon quickly and completely converted the book-selling business. Time to say good-bye, Borders.

Not only did Amazon excel in the book-selling business, it also went on to create a reliable online retail experience that customers can't live without. Now Amazon is the largest online retailer in the world, and has one of the largest and rapidly growing Web Services division, and it all happened with lightning speed.

Netflix began sending DVDs to people's homes and completely disrupted the in-store video rental business of Blockbuster. Now Netflix has reinvented itself again, streaming video content on demand, and it even creates some of that content itself.

Think about that for a moment. Netflix has pivoted from DVD retailer, to streaming content, to TV and movie producer. Two pivot points that have transformed their business, and is transforming their industry. Now Netflix is looking to expand globally and stream content to the far reaches of the world and to capture viewer reactions by creating content that appeals to specific viewer tastes.

New entrants are on the scene and trying to eat Netflix's business for lunch. Hulu and Amazon Prime, to name just two, are challenging the business model. Netflix is having to reinvent itself again and credits its culture for its ability to adapt quickly. This is the way of the twenty-first-century world.

Quick reinvention can't be done in the sleepy, highly controlled environments of the traditional organizations of the past. Speed and creativity with more readily available data are the bywords of this century's organizations. Leading companies today are realizing they can't unleash the creativity of their employees with slow, bureaucratic cultures.

THE EVOLUTION OF CULTURE

Culture first started being discussed as an element of the workplace in the early 1970s and 1980s. Leading researchers began looking at the hidden elements of what they were calling "culture" and its impact on organizational performance.

Despite the revolutionary discussions of culture, it was still very much a fringe or soft study. Typical of organizations of the day, managers and leaders did not want to talk about the emotional, human side of business. Leaders often steered clear of discussions about trust, values, relationships, and cooperation. They were simply not prepared for this type of discussion.

Business schools did not emphasize the "people factors." Shareholder value was the Holy Grail. Empirical proof that culture would have an impact on a business's bottom line was required, but not sought.

Exercises we did in the early 1980s asked business focus groups how they treated people they trusted, and did not trust, at work. The results were clear: they shared information and ideas with those they trusted. Team members were more helpful when their trusted coworkers needed assistance, and they were allies to these people from a career perspective.

They tended to avoid and not share information or ideas with those they did not trust. Given the opportunity, they would throw untrusted colleagues under the bus. It was obvious from the discussion that culture—how people related to each other and made decisions together—was a critical success factor for an organization.

Yet, in the hard-boiled business world there were many doubting Thomases who believed that the industrial era concepts about how their workers interacted should prevail. Workers should come to work, do their jobs, and get paid.

Money was the principle bargaining chip for performance, and employee satisfaction was not considered in achieving business goals.

UNDERSTANDING CULTURE

We and other researchers began to codify culture and create instruments to measure it. As a result, consistent elements of organizational culture became clearer. Certain cultures drove certain business results.

Businesses that embraced the importance of organizational culture in the early days, such as Southwest Airlines, were showing strong growth. Their employees were engaged, worked to delight the customers, and solved problems in their work arenas.

Compare Southwest's culture to that of General Motors. The contrast is startling and the results are clear. GM was struggling with integrity violations, consumer trust issues, and market share erosion, whereas Southwest is lauded as a customer-focused, employee-centric organization that empowers its staff to take initiative in how they deliver their service. With a focus on culture, and more important, changing their culture, GM is now lauded by Fast Company as one of the "biggest business comeback stories in the last 20 years." Culture Matters.

Quantification of culture proved there was a strong correlation between employee-focused cultures and organizational performance. Toward the end of the twentieth century, culture was recognized as a key factor for success. Thought leaders like Peter Drucker were talking about how culture eats strategy for lunch.

FAST-FORWARD CULTURE

Fast-forward to today. Job markets are changing rapidly, with fewer factory workers and more knowledge workers. More entry-level employees have different expectations, are technologically savvy, and want to work on meaningful projects. Companies like Google, Facebook, and PwC are the new normal. These companies know they can't be fast and flexible with cultures rooted in industrial thinking.

Kodak died because of a complacent culture that missed where the market was going. This was also the case for Blockbuster and RIM (now reborn as BlackBerry Limited). The two areas that worry CEOs the most, according to recent PwC studies, are talent and technological disruption. Culture is a critical part of both of these concerns.

Companies must be fast, but they also have to be flexible learning organizations where innovation can happen quickly—in every part of the organization, not just in the places where the research is done. And execution must be flawless.

Today, culture is a key consideration in leadership hiring. There is hardly a merger or acquisition of any size where cultural impact and cohesion is not discussed. Many companies have failed and failed quickly due to a poor cultural fit. In fact, many companies have hired senior executives from other companies to help change their culture only to have them fail because dysfunction was so entrenched.

Spencer Stuart and other recruitment firms cite a 45 percent executive fail rate attributable to a poor cultural fit. When the new executive tries to do things differently, the cultural antibodies take over and push him out.

One senior leader in a Fortune 100 company we were working with shared how she was struggling in her current position. She stated the challenge of not being able to move any proposals forward as they were always being criticized. She didn't know what to do.

In exploring this challenge further, it became very clear that the environment she was looking for was not the environment she was in. She ultimately resigned at a great cost to the company. In seeking a new position, she paid attention to the culture and was hired by a competitor. She is thriving to this day. This story highlights the crucial importance of the human element—the way people interact and the relationships they build—to the success of the organization.

Cultures that are toxic by their very nature are not innovative. People in these toxic organizations lay low, stay out of trouble, and rarely step forward with an innovative idea or recommendation.

If you're not purposely investing in a healthy culture, your business is already declining, whether you realize it or not.

THE VALUES AND CULTURE CONNECTION

Culture is rooted in values. Not the ones on the posters in the hallways but in the values that really shape the practices of the organization.

Notice the beautiful value statements on the walls: *We are a team. We work to bring great solutions to our customers. Our people are our most important asset. Integrity is our core.*

But when you ask for help, you get bounced around.

While flying on a very reputable airline, we encountered challenges getting access to Wi-Fi and asked the attendant for help. He said he didn't know how to get access to Wi-Fi because "they [staff] weren't allowed to use it." What was particularly poignant about his comment was that the CEO of the company had just been on the video monitor talking about how much the company valued its great team of people.

Clearly this attendant missed that value in his day-to-day experience. Interestingly, that CEO was recently fired.

We were chatting recently with Josh Bersin, of Bersin and Associates, about his firm's research that pointed in the same compelling direction. He and his team reviewed 6,000 companies on Glassdoor representing more than 2.2 million employees. They discovered, as did we, that culture and company values were the biggest driver of a company's brand.

Our own study of over 500 Fortune 1,000 companies showed that culture and values statistically had the greatest impact on the company's brand and market performance, followed by coaching and learning.

BRINGING CULTURE TO LIGHT

Culture comprises the unspoken rules that guide people every day, not the policy manuals or the organization charts that depict how things are supposed to get done in an imaginary world.

It's the unspoken set of assumptions, values, and beliefs that dictate, often subtly, how people relate to each other in organizations. These shared values have a strong influence on how people dress, act, and perform their jobs. It defines how people in the organization think about their work and contribute to the overall organization.

While we were working with employees from a famous Silicon Valley company, one senior leader told us this story. He came to Silicon Valley from the company's London office, which had a more formal dress code. He wore cufflinks, dress shirts, and gray flannel pants, and he happened to like how he dressed.

After his transfer to the Silicon Valley office, the human resource leader kept telling him there wasn't a dress code at this office. So he kept dressing as he always had, simply taking the comment at face value. After repeated statements by the human resource manager regarding no dress code, he turned to the HR leader and said, "Apparently there is, as you all want me to dress like you." It was true, there was pressure to conform to this company's Silicon Valley cultural value of dressing informally.

We had the pleasure of working with John Mattone, a best-selling author with his latest book, *Cultural Transformations*. We were speaking in Mexico, sharing notes and debating our perspective on culture and values. This quote from Mattone sums up the substance of culture.

Culture is the collective character, values, thoughts, emotions, beliefs, and behaviors of your leaders and individual contributors. Your organization's culture is a product of such factors as its history and how your leaders and individual contributors ascribe meaning and value to it, as well as leadership style (legacy and current), which is then reflected in the creation and implementation of your organization's values, vision, mission, purpose, strategy, structure, and roles.

As we like to put it—it's the DNA of a company that happens whether you want it or not.

It's really not about what gets done but how it gets done. To put it another way, it's one of the top three things a company becomes known for.

Culture shapes how employees act, not only with each other but also with the customer. It informs how decisions are ultimately made about everything from who you hire and reward to how you shape strategy and execute it. Culture is everything.

We recently spoke with Mike Derezin, vice president of sales solutions at LinkedIn, about workplace culture. He related,

> Culture is who we are and who we aspire to be, and values that we articulate are the set of guiding principles that help guide us in making decisions on a day-to-day basis. We have five cultural tenants and we have six values, but those are paramount to how we run the business.
>
> Culture is going to form whether you like it or not so, you may as well take control of it and shape it the way you want.
>
> If your employees are engaged and they have the right fit and they love your culture, what are they going to do? They're going to tell their friends all about it naturally, and their colleagues and other people they respect. And now you have an inbound flow of talent.
>
> It's very valuable when you're trying to make strategic moves and decisions and establish shared language so high-quality and speedy decisions can be made.

Hamptonality™ is the word used at Hampton Inns to describe their culture. When we were talking to their HR leader in charge of culture, he acknowledged that the hotel industry is a commodity business. They have to compete on the culture they create in the workforce.

If hotels want customers to return time and time again in a highly commoditized business, they have to create a special buzz. What makes Hampton Inn different is the culture. Employees at every level are empowered to make the customer experience great and have a budget they can tap into to go above and beyond.

For example, a frequent guest missed his plane and was coming in very late. The desk clerk knew he would not be able to get dinner and would be hungry. The desk clerk went to this customer's favorite burger place, bought him a burger and his favorite drink, and had it in his room upon arrival.

A cleaning lady knew a mother was arriving with her three-year-old son and made animal shapes out to the hand towels, much to the boy's delight.

These examples are not costly, but they are caring actions that show the staff is trying to make a great customer experience. The culture Hampton Inn is cultivating is this: *customers really do matter!*

Zappos is famous for the culture it created and how it achieved it. Zappos has a holocracy manifesto that employees write and agree to. It's a living document that is discussed, reviewed, and signed by each employee. Culture is so important to this company that all meetings and discussions begin with their cultural values.

We had the pleasure of interviewing Jason Carthen, an NFL Super Bowl winner. In his career, Jason has seen a number of parallels between corporate culture and the organizational dynamics of sports teams. In particular, one experience on the football field has stuck with him.

While running a play during practice, one of his teammates lost a shoe. The young man kept right on playing, but when the play was over, the coach berated him in the harshest possible terms. The player said, "You don't have to talk to me like that."

The coach got in the player's face, lambasted him, and yelled at him to get off the field.

Not only was the individual cut from the team, but he was labeled a problem player, and another team that had expressed interest in him withdrew its offer.

"He never played again," Jason said. "It was tough, because he wasn't a problem. He was a good guy. He was trying to stand up for himself. It just showed that when you have a toxic culture, that culture will either build a champion or hide a hero."

We can relate to this because we've seen many CEOs berate their people in public because they think it makes them look strong. And it doesn't, not at all. Instead, they're driving their people to operate on the basis of fear. And when people are fearful, they don't do their best.

Jason agreed. "If you're leading by fear, people are going to hedge," he said. "They're going to do just enough to not get fired, but passive-aggressively they'll let you know they have not bought into the vision."

Sir Clive Woodward, a successful English rugby coach, takes a very different coaching approach with his team. While at a conference in Dubai, we had the good fortune to meet Clive and interview him later for the radio show. Clive shared how he helps shape his team's talent.

They review footage from previous games and note both the good plays and the bad ones. This system of coaching has created a culture of learning, not fear, and a culture of making sure each player is playing his best.

Clive would show footage of the plays and then encourage a dialogue among the players about what they could change. They listen to each other and learn from each other. He merely facilitates the discussion. The proof of this approach is certainly evident in the success of the team, which went on to win the world cup.

The Queen knighted him Sir Clive Woodward. Clive's cultural values were to bring out the best in others and help people learn. He did this through his actions, and he never deviated from his values.

We had the pleasure of talking with Rich Sheriden, CEO of Menlo Innovations and author of *Joy Inc*. We discussed our career experiences and what drove Rich to create the working environment he did at Menlo.

He told us he experienced joyless organizations most of his working life and wanted to turn those experiences around. So, he decided to create an organization that valued joy at work. He has been resoundingly successful. Walk into his organization and you can feel the joy.

Rich also shared about Menlo's thin management structure and highly democratic approach to work. Two values of the company are family time and personal well-being. Menlo has established a culture of working only 40 hours a week and never working on weekends. The company never denies a vacation request. Rich himself sticks to the company's values, and his assistant completely shuts off his e-mail and contact with the office when he's on vacation. He did confess that this practice was challenging at first.

Tanfeeth, the UAE outsourcing company introduced in Chapter 2, has an employee-centered culture. We talked to CEO Suhail Bin Tarraf about how the company culture is shaped and what he does to ensure the well-being of the workforce.

Suhail said he believes that each employee has a right to health and to learn and grow. As we shared earlier, he believes that you can't be effective if you are stressed about something at home, or are distracted by family issues. Another interesting benefit of the morning discussion is that team members will talk about and share, what they learned from customers the day before that could be helpful to others.

Employees are also encouraged to express if they are sad or stressed or have something that is causing them pressure. If necessary, they may choose to leave work that day. Other team members fill in and help out. Since they have a healthy culture, no one abuses this approach and the employees support each other as needed, knowing that everyone will, at somepoint, need the teams' support.

Bin Tarraf's leadership style encourages others to share their feelings. As a result, a company culture was created that supports the needs of the business and as well as the needs of each employee.

It's not the twentieth-century culture that valued business first over employees. Instead it's a twenty-first-century culture that embraces both.

Working with Suhail and his team was a chance to see upfront how he created joy at work.

How Do You Create a Culture That Hums?

Culture is king for the twenty-first century. Successful companies are breaking all the rules we believed in the past about how companies need to be run. This means fewer rules, more trust, and more freedom for employees to unleash their intelligence and gifts, no matter what role they play in the organization.

Know your current culture. Understand it not as you would like it to be but as it really is. Get the true facts about the current culture and face the reality even if you don't like it. If you don't like everything you see, it's time to make a serious change.

Define what the culture and values of the organization must be. Then use those values to guide all your business decisions.

A senior executive of a health care organization told us his story of facing the biggest crisis in his company's history. He decided to be true to the values of his company and not base all his decisions on the finances. Despite enormous pressures, he took a deep breath and used the company's values to guide the next steps.

He said this choice was the most important decision he ever made for the company. By using the company's values as the standard for action, his team came up with a completely different approach to making strategic decisions, and it saved his company.

Now they always start any initiative with values as their strategic guide.

HARD CHOICES

When working with a very famous hospital, we found the leaders would consistently accept bad behavior from employees considered indispensable. The departments were led by leaders who did not live the values of the hospital. They were losing staff and found it difficult to recruit new replacements because the word was out about the hospital's toxic culture.

The CEO, after careful reflection, decided his leaders' support of the hospital's values was more important than their brilliant reputations. He had the courage to stand up to the board and make the right talent calls to remove the bad apples. To everyone's delight, this hospital not only survived—without these toxic leaders—it thrived.

Never reward or promote anyone who does not live the values of the enterprise. Rewarding or promoting an individual who does not live the values of the organization will erode the underlying well-being of your company's culture, regardless of all the good that all your other actions promoted.

LEADING A FUTURE-PROOF CULTURE

So how does a company, or division, crystalize its values and create a future-proof culture?

Start by assessing your own personal values and answering the question: *What is the culture our company needs to execute a successful strategy?*

Daydream about what that would look like. *This type of culture is what we need to enjoy the successes we want. This is why we exist as a company.*

Then look at the behaviors you see every day—in your staff and yourself. Identify the disconnect and begin to articulate the values you aspire to in order to have the success you envision.

Instead of blaming others, get honest data, psychometric surveys, and 360-degree assessments that can point to what the current culture is and what it needs to be to go where you want to go.

Yes, people often blame leaders, but you can look at the culture in your department and become a shining star in a sea of mediocrity.

We worked with an HR leader in a global business based in Europe. The overall company culture was unhealthy, and the numbers showed it. But the HR leader took a hard look at the culture in her department and made changes. In two years the department became a recognized top performer in company, attracting the attention of leaders in the company headquarters who asked what she had done to create the positive results.

We also see common missteps when leaders try to improve culture. These include not taking personal ownership for cultural change but delegating it to a program or outsourcing it to HR and not modeling the culture the leaders say they want. Most harmful of all, they let people get away with words and actions that are contrary to company values.

As the old saying goes, actions speak louder than words. We imagine this saying originated *not* in the boardroom but in the break room.

Cultivating a healthy culture is non-negotiable for a leader, and some would argue it's the primary role.

The examples of courageous leaders putting values into action should convince you that you can do it too.

Leaders create the culture that they love.

The future-proof culture is one that everyone can love.

FUTURE-PROOF YOUR COMPANY

- Look for signs of an unhealthy culture like negative engagement surveys and customer complaints. That's when future-thinking leaders admit there's a problem and look for solutions.

- Discuss how you and your teams have lived the values in the past six months and how you plan to live them in the next six months.

- Cultural problems often masquerade as tech issues or people problems. Stop rearranging deck chairs on the *Titanic*. Quality problems are always the result of unhealthy culture.

Future-Proof Your Career

- Crystalize your personal values and embody them at work. Decide which personal values overlap company values and model them with your peers. Create a peer culture that will be an example for others.

- Give colleagues permission to call you out when they see actions that don't reflect company values.

CHAPTER 4

Purpose

Navigating Turbulent Waters

> Those who spend their lives searching for
> happiness never find it, while those who search for
> meaning, purpose, and strong personal
> relationships find that happiness usually comes to
> them as a by-product of those three things.
>
> —Nido R. Qubein, President of High Point University

Remember the good old days when the first thing you had to do as a leader was create a mission statement so employees and customers understood the business that you were in?

Then you had to have a great vision statement, often bordering on science fiction and designed to draw the company and its people forward.

Then the next step was to create yearly goals to move toward the vision. Dashboards to track the goals were a must, and the years churned on and on in that fashion.

Just about every company in the developed world employed these tools and techniques. Consultants and teams spent days and weeks trying to craft just the right statements. These statements often became long and unwieldy, lacking any emotional inspiration for anyone!

The irony was that these statements were supposed to be marketplace differentiators. They were supposed to excite customers and energize employees. And these meager phrases were intended to guide the daily activities of a work group, and an entire company, throughout the year. All work and performance would be measured against them. And yet, no one could ever remember them.

We could wrap our companies, and our work, with nice, predictable bows. Progress would happen in incremental and linear ways. All we had to do was execute against our goals, track progress, and show results. Business life was good. Sure, we had contingency plans just in case things shifted a bit. This was a typical yearly planning and strategy cycle.

As we reminisce about the twentieth-century workplace, those good old days seems so *passé* or "meh" in today's lexicon.

MISSION AND VISION

Here are some examples of mission and vision statements. Not only do they seem archaic, but they are wrapped in so much corporate-speak that few can make sense of their intention.

Apple Computer

We believe that we are on the face of the earth to make great products and that's not changing. We are constantly focusing on innovating. We believe in the simple not the complex. We believe that we need to own and control the primary technologies behind the products that we make, and participate only in markets where we can make a significant contribution. We believe in saying no to thousands of projects, so that we can really focus on the few that are truly important and meaningful to us. We believe in deep collaboration and cross-pollination of our groups, which allow us to innovate in a way that others cannot. And frankly, we don't settle for anything less than excellence in every group in the company, and we have the self-honesty to admit when we're wrong and the courage to change. And I think regardless of who is in what job those values are so embedded in this company that Apple will do extremely well.

—*Tim Cook, CEO of Apple Computer (Quoted on CNN Money.com)*

Avon

"Avon's mission is focused on six core aspirations the company continually strives to achieve," begins Avon's mission statement. Then it goes on. And on. It weighs in at 249 words that cover everything from surpassing competitors to increasing shareholder value to fighting breast cancer.[1]

These statements are meaningless and boring to people who were not personally involved in their development—which is just about everyone on the planet. They don't differentiate, excite, or compel people to act, whether the reader is an employee or a potential customer.

But some funny things happened on the way to the forum that changed all of this forever.

In the twenty-first century, work can shift in nanoseconds and complicated missions can become obsolete overnight, based on many factors discussed in this book. The days of occasional whitewater for a company have given way to perpetual rapids with hidden rocks all along the way.

Typical ways of strategic planning and execution were made for more predictable days on calmer waters.

Work that used to take years now happens in days.

WHAT ARE WE BUILDING?

In recent discussions with Rita McGrath, a leading expert on strategy, she put it this way. The strategies and processes that were originally put in place to provide "maximum value from a competitive advantage, become a liability when the environment requires the capacity to surf through waves of short-lived opportunities."

In other words, instead of building a ship to sail with the changing tides, companies often build massive management machinery that can't move, gets swamped by change, and rusts.

Kodak believed that photos would always be film based. AT&T believed that people would always use landlines. Leading tech companies believed that tablets and PCs would always be the norm. In fact, tablet sales are down 22 percent this year, and the trend is expected to continue.

These companies were structured with lofty sounding missions and visions, and what seemed like disciplined strategy development and execution. But it was these very systems, processes, and beliefs that put them in jeopardy.

In the twentieth century these processes and operating disciplines were often heralded as game-changing. But when the strategies and tactics were not monitored and adjusted for changing conditions, leaders mistook the crash of the iceberg against the hull for applause.

Leaders created cultures of complacency and bureaucracy where the processes became more important than the outcomes and marketplace impact. *After all*, they thought, *we have decades to get things right.*

When Linda was working at General Electric (GE), it invested in RIM. It was a cutting-edge company and moving fast. Of course, RIM provided all the GE executives with Black-Berrys and everyone got hooked.

RIM regularly made great improvements in the BlackBerry and life was good. People couldn't live without their BlackBerrys. The company was making record profits, and GE made its investment back in spades.

But then came the smartphones, touchscreens, and all the bells and whistles. Sadly, RIM could not keep up. Its culture had become complacent with its success. The competition, which never got the memo about innovation taking years to move through the hierarchy, was simply too fast for a methodic organization like RIM.

Contrast this with Amazon, which started out as an online retailer, simply selling printed books. That was it. And then it morphed and stretched into a massive online juggernaut. Who ever thought that Amazon would be the biggest retailer and the largest cloud storage company in the world?

Not Walmart. Or Kmart. Or Borders.

Now Amazon produces movies and curates news. Here is its mission statement:

"To be the Earth's most customer-centric company, where customers can find and discover anything they might want to buy online."

Why is Amazon so successful? How has it navigated so much technological change and market turmoil?

One main difference is that it has a compelling purpose that drives all other strategies, tactics, and activities: Deliver what the customers want to buy, when and where they want it. You can count on Amazon to deliver whatever you order—whether it's a phone, a book, a can of organic chicken soup, or a cute dress that you need this weekend—in its trademark box to your doorstep. Taking that to the next level, Amazon recently announced a partnership with Goodwill where customers could repack their Amazon delivery box with items for donation and then have these shipped for free to Goodwill. Innovation that links directly to purpose, reinforces culture, and informs leadership behavior.

In another scenario, Amazon could have continued to serve only customers who wanted printed books. It could have done that well and never even changed the game with e-books. But it chose a greater purpose.

Markets change.

Technology disrupts.

Culture evolves.

People learn.

Relationships grow.

Purpose remains.

Old-fashioned planning and mission statements do nothing to propel a company forward in today's markets. Dump them and replace them with a simple purpose statement.

A clear purpose statement unleashes the intellect of employees to meet the needs of team members and customers.

PURPOSE

Greg Ellis, former CEO and managing director of REA Group, said his company's purpose was "to make the process simple, efficient, and stress-free for people buying and selling property."

This takes outward focus to a whole new level, not just emphasizing the importance of serving customers or understanding their needs but also putting managers and employees in the customers' shoes. It's outward-focused: *This is what we're doing for someone else.* And the purpose is motivational because it connects with the heart as well as the head. Indeed, Ellis called it the company's "philosophical heartbeat."[2]

This embodies the difference a compelling purpose can make. It is an outside-in view of what the company does.

Purpose begins with the promise to customers—not giving the customers everything they want but rather living up to the promise they make to customers.

As Dave Ulrich, Rensis Likert professor at the Ross School of Business, University of Michigan, a partner at The RBL Group, and a thought leader in human resources put it in our recent conversation, what makes the difference today is being clear on your promise to the customer. Having a customer-centric view ensures you are delivering on what you say you will deliver.

The best purpose statements are timeless and adjust with changing technology and changing circumstances. They are inspiring, as in "providing clean water for all the people in the world." Not only is this stirring, but it guides behavior. *Is what I am doing going to help create clean water for people, and if not, why am I doing it?* It helps create clear direction.

But an effective purpose also has another very important role: to create an authentic emotional hook for the betterment of society.

PURPOSE IS INSPIRING

We know from studying the brain that emotion creates a strong motivational factor for people, which, in turn, promotes action. Purpose aligns people's behaviors around something that makes a difference to others.

Contrast this with this statement from famed former CEO, Jack Welsh, of GE. Jack's mantra was the much-touted "be number one or two in the market."

Jack used this phrase consistently to guide GE's impressive market growth. No question this mantra was followed by many in the 1990s. And think about this statement from the CEO of a very large tech company. His organizing vision for his company was to achieve billions of dollars in revenues by 2020. While this vision was compelling on one level, it certainly was not inspiring and definitely did not create an emotional hook. This vision was completely market-driven, not customer-driven, and did not impel employees to support the greater good.

The GE mantra engaged the head—the logic of the statement is unquestionable. But purpose engages the head and the heart and aligns emotion with the logic, a powerful combination for inspiring a rallying cry.

A command and control leadership style, coupled with a focus on greed, causes questionable practices that actually hurt people.

Add a mission statement that is solely market-driven, and you have the perfect storm for corruption.

If your guiding directive is to make money, you and your team may do that at all costs because that, presumably, is what will be rewarded. The lofty mission and vision statements will continue to be ignored because they are already being ignored.

The CEO of a very large tech company, who we were working with, insisted that the *raison d'etre* of his company was the $3 billion number. In every meeting he harped on the fact that this was the goal. How uninspiring, financially driven, and completely disconnected from the customer.

Who gets excited about a number? Robots and artificial intelligence aficionados we suppose, but that's another chapter.

The reason GE continued to thrive was, and is, the strong values the company embraced deeply in its culture.

THE POWER OF PURPOSE

Today there are more than 2 billion people under 20 years of age in the world. These are people who will be in our workforce shortly, and many are already here. In fact, over 45 percent of the workforce is millennials. Why is this important?

These 2 billion people have a different drummer that motivates them. We have raised children to give back and to be less compelled by making vast amounts of money at others' expense.

We were raised by people who survived the Great Depression and two catastrophic world wars, which shaped a greater perceived need for personal security. That motivation has changed.

Linda recently had the pleasure of meeting Jared Kleinert, an impressive millennial who coauthored the book *2 Billion Under 20* with Stacey Ferreira.

When she first saw the title of the book, Linda mistakenly thought that he made 2 billion dollars before he was 20 years old. We'll talk about unconscious bias and preconceptions later in this book.

Jared is on a mission to counter the view that millennials are mostly selfish, whiny young people who have to be coddled.

He asked millennials to share stories of what they were working on, and the stories are amazing. Linda's first reaction was great admiration for these young people and for what they are doing. Some of their efforts failed the first time, but they kept trying and did amazing things. But here is the defining feature of what all these young people did.

They were motivated by a compelling purpose for the greater good.

These folks were working on ideas that would solve world-wide problems. In particular, Jared pointed out that millennials were not interested in making widgets better or improving process. They were interested in solving "big, hairy problems" that plague mankind.

All the many actions these young people take on are geared to a noble purpose and will make the world a better place. Aspirational, perhaps, but nonetheless awe-inspiring.

If companies are to attract these young people, they must also have an awe-inspiring purpose.

Purpose and People

Mike Derezin, VP of sales solutions for LinkedIn, recently shared his thoughts about purpose:

> We really try to explain that we are here for this purpose. We're a mission-driven company and for us to achieve our mission and our vision we obviously need revenue and profits, but those are actually secondary. We're here for far more than just to make money.
>
> Purpose is meaning, and we all want meaning, so I think it obviously hits the very core of who we all are as humans. But one of the reasons that's increasingly important is if you look at a lot of studies and conversations with millennials they over-index on purpose far more than other generations.
>
> For example, you could take an industry like insurance. Is the real way to rally your team around revenue goals for the year? Or to start with a very personal story of what the insurance company did to help some of their policy holders? Lead with that and then go into, "now, how do you get there?"

In the twentieth century, people came into work, but their emotional purpose was outside the workplace—usually back at home.

In the twenty-first century it's the emotional purpose that causes people to *come* to work.

BANKING ON PURPOSE

Here is an example of how a staid bank turned itself into a powerful force for its customers by methodically articulating a powerful purpose statement and values.

Right from the start, the company strove to identify its values. "I wanted to make sure we thought about what we stood for as a company," said Margaret M. Keane, President and CEO of Synchrony Financial. "And more importantly, how do we take what we saw as the good things of GE, bring those forward, and then create our own vision and purpose for our company? So I embarked on this very early in the IPO process. I felt it was very important that the organization rallied around and felt good about our purpose and our values."

Crafting their purpose statement was a team effort, involving input from customers, the leadership team, and employees throughout the entire company. The process was labor-intensive, but Margaret said, "It was something I felt strongly about—that in order for us to come out of the gate as a strong, highly valued company, having a purpose and values that we believed in was really important to us as an organization."

Their statement still guides company activities every day, Margaret told Linda. "We've been rolling this out across the whole company and in various unique and fun ways."

For example, an intra-company profile website encourages employees to post images of how they're living their favorite values. "I think it's really working to show how those values are coming alive inside the company."

Linda was impressed when she walked into Synchrony Financial's office and saw statements from employees and customers on video. The testimonials showcased how Synchrony helped them with a particular life crisis. Nowhere did she see platitudes from the leaders, and especially not Margaret, telling us how great the company is.

Instead, the company's purpose statement was on full display, in words and actions: "Our purpose is to pioneer the future of financing, improving the success of every business we serve and the quality of each life we touch."

Contrast this with the many CEOs that we see in airplanes talking about how great their company is and how big it is now that it has merged. Nothing exudes from these pronouncements except that big equals money.

This is particularly frustrating when we miss a connection that the airlines could have avoided or experience horrible customer service from people who couldn't care less that we could not get home after a long workweek.

We met Lisa McLeod, author of *Leading with Noble Purpose*, at a recent authors' summit where she was interviewing our friend, Marshall Goldsmith.

Lisa had always been in sales and worked with salespeople all over the world. She shared this story about a saleswoman she had worked with.

"The sales person got to know a patient that had a very rare and tough form of an illness. She had been introduced to the patient by the physician who was treating her. This salesperson jumped through hoops to get a medication to this woman who would have suffered if she did not have it. The salesperson saw it not as a sales role to sell the drug but as her purpose to ensure this woman had what she needed. She saw in her role a greater purpose—helping to save this woman's life."

This changed everything for her. This made her job intensely meaningful. It changed the whole dynamic of what she did every day from making money to helping people in need. This is the essence of purpose-driven organizations—and purpose-driven people.

Purpose is powerful. It appeals to our inner need as humans to contribute to the greater good.

What is your real purpose on earth?

Ours is to build great leaders and organizations so everyone can thrive.

It can be hard to live your purpose 100 percent of the time, we are human after all, but good leaders strive to do so. And great leaders regularly reflect on how well they are aligned with, and living, their purpose and make changes accordingly.

Purpose is a leadership journey, not a destination.

On the organizational level, do you really believe the values you put forward?

What is the greater good you and your company provide to the customer?

What would customers say is really your brand—not the brand your marketing people are trying to make others to believe.

FUTURE-PROOF YOUR COMPANY

- Does your company have a relevant purpose? Or are you coasting on motivations left over from the previous century? Dare to take down those tired placards and replace them with a simple, compelling purpose.

- How do current initiatives stack up beside your purpose? Where are the connects and disconnects?

- Is your purpose future-focused and adaptable?

- Do you hold everyone, especially your leaders, accountable for walking the talk and living that purpose? Or do you tolerate toxic behaviors and bad apples because of the results they deliver despite the cost?

FUTURE-PROOF YOUR CAREER

- Have you really examined why you work? Yes, we know it is to support your family and strive for a better life. But how do you define *your* better life? Is it values-based or money-based?

- On a personal level, dig deep for your compelling values. What is the legacy you want to leave, and what is it you want to be remembered for? This may sound trite, but it is an important reflection point. As our good friend Marshall Goldsmith often asks, "When you're 90 years old on your deathbed, what do you want to be remembered for? Is it that $30 million of cost you took out or the people you helped achieve their dreams?"

- Have a five-minute call with a colleague every week. Share your values and purpose with each other and ask, "Have I behaved consistently with my values and purpose?" If not, what can you do next week to drive more consistency?

CHAPTER 5

Relationships

Our Connected Future

> No man is an island entire unto itself.
> Each is a piece of the continent, a part
> of the main.
>
> —John Donne

Business is built on relationships, whether with employees, with customers, or with other key stakeholders.

You cannot be successful in business, or in life, unless you are also successful in cultivating the personal and professional relationships on which these depend. The organizations and individuals who successfully navigate this new work order are those who are paying attention to how work gets done—by building effective relationships.

And no, there's not an app for that.

Building relationships still happens the old-fashioned way, one conversation and one interaction at a time. It's the human to human connection from which everything else builds.

We are in a transition phase in terms of how relationships are valued in the workplace. The percentage of workers who come from the traditional "business is business" mind-set is still large. However, as they approach retirement age, the next generation of workers is stepping forward and the pace of change will accelerate.

The future of work will center on the fluid workforce. This fluid workforce consists of teams and individuals who can come together rapidly, build trust, enable information sharing, and collaborate to deliver a successful result.

Yes, technology plays a major role in team communication, but the more things change, the more things stay the same. Business is personal. If you believe your company or career can rely on technology to minimize the importance of relationships, you're in for a future shock.

The workplace of the future will be a different environment than what has served us to date. Our professional relationships will also need to flex. The shifting nature of work relationships creates opportunities and challenges for employers and employees alike.

"Relationships are shifting and suddenly there is far more intimacy in the workplace than there used to be before," said Anat Lechner, clinical associate professor of management and organizations at New York University Stern School of Business.[1]

In this chapter we will explore how our relationships with work, and at work, are changing in five key areas:

1. Work

2. Employer

3. Colleagues

4. Network

5. Community

We will also provide steps you can take today to future-proof your company and your career.

A TALE OF TWO PARTS: MORAG'S STORY

Before we explore the five relationship areas of work, we want to set the scene and demonstrate how relationships at work have already evolved in both striking and subtle ways.

Part 1: 1986

The alarm rang shrilly, breaking the dream I was having. I leaned over to switch off the noise. It was 6:30 AM. I never was a morning person. Time to get up, shower, dress, and find something for breakfast. I read the newspaper and had a quick stab at the crossword before I got in my car and drove to work.

As the newest member on staff, my responsibilities were clear: Unlock the bank branch, switch on the lights and computer (which was the size of a desk), and make sure the kettle was on. When the bank manager arrived, it was my job to bring his cup of tea.

The doors to the branch opened at 10 AM and that's usually when the first customer would arrive. The tellers manually stamped the checks and deposit slips and passed them back for processing. My day was spent at the computer entering bank account information and the amounts of each item.

There was banter across the team of 15 in this small branch. Although we were part of a national bank, we rarely met with our colleagues at the nearest branch. It was only 15 miles away, but it may as well have been on the other side of the planet. Business was conducted locally. Relationships were only maintained with our day-to-day colleagues and the customers who lived and worked in our town.

The loan officer processed the new applications for personal loans and reviewed the checking accounts that were overdrawn. The loan applications were credit-scored by hand against an internal document: 10 points for having a phone, zero points for not having a car.

A few customers exceeded their overdraft limits. A phone call to the head office, and a conversation with a colleague in another city who we'd never met, determined if the overdraft limit would be increased or if the check would bounce.

When the doors closed at 3 PM, I finished the processing by adding the magnetic ink character recognition code to each item, bundled each item, and put them into a sealed bag for the security van to pick them up.

At 5 PM I headed home. The day was done. Just another busy day at the office.

Part 2: 2017

The alarm played out the refrain from my favorite artist and broke into yet another dream I was enjoying. I still don't like mornings, but today I need to move quickly.

The first conference call starts at 6:30 AM. It's now 5:30 AM, as I quickly check my phone, delete the marketing e-mails, and consider responses to client e-mails for later in the day. Time to get up, shower, dress, and gulp breakfast before heading downstairs to my home office.

The video conference starts promptly with participants from Italy and London on the line. We start with some laughter and catch up on our weekend adventures. One of my colleagues had a family reunion, so we spend time sharing our stories and anecdotes. It's fun and relaxed, and while I've never met these people in person, it feels like we've known each other for years.

We've been collaborating for nearly six months, designing a leadership program that will be launching in the next few weeks. We leverage technology to see each other and share the documents we have been working on. Collaboration is quick, and it's easy.

Call over. I jump in the car and immediately the phone rings (hands free connection, of course!). I have a chat with a coaching client who needs immediate advice on how to handle a difficult conversation later in the day. The day continues with a facilitated event at a client's office followed by a brief meeting to agree on next steps. Now I can head home . . . to work.

I sit on the sofa, the e-mails have continued to arrive all day and now is my time to respond. The TV is on, and I multitask as I reply to each inquiry and think about what I need for the next day. It's not time to completely relax; one more telephone conference call has been scheduled for 9 PM local time to accommodate the clients based in Singapore and Sydney.

The day finally ends at 11 PM.

RELATIONSHIP WITH WORK

These two short vignettes are very real—and very different. They demonstrate how, in a few short years, the relationships we experience at work, and with work, have changed. We've moved from a local perspective to a global perspective. Our relationship with the workday, and work itself, has expanded from the 9 to 5 to the 24/7.

Let's be honest. Work is at the center of most of our lives. It's the necessary evil for many that allows us to pay the bills. And for those exceptional few, work is a place where we thrive and actually look forward to being. (Yes, those scenarios exist!)

In fact, we propose that the reason so many people dread work is because they've avoided the important step of cultivating good relationships in the workplace.

Work is where we form many of our most treasured relationships, whether it's friends and colleagues or potential spouses. It's also where we uncover and refine the relationship we develop with ourselves. When this all goes well, we thrive and creativity and innovation abound. We feel connected when we're adding value and contributing expertise to a positive result. We have purpose.

On the other side of the coin, when our relationship with work, or relationships at work, flounder, we can find ourselves stressed, withholding our knowledge, and taking those stressors home to our families and friends. When our professional relationships are damaged, this invariably impacts our personal relationships.

Work matters, and the world of work is probably the biggest team sport any of us get to participate in. As a team sport, business can't be just about the numbers.

We don't have to look far to understand why our relationship to work needs to change. A Google search for the definition of work resulted in this:

Work/werk/[2]
Noun: activity involving mental or physical effort done in order to achieve a purpose or result. "He was tired after a day's work in the fields."

Synonyms: labor, toil, slog, drudgery, exertion, effort, industry, service; informal grind, sweat, elbow grease

verb: be engaged in physical or mental activity in order to achieve a purpose or result, especially in one's job; do work. "An engineer had been working on a design for a more efficient wing."

synonyms: toil, labor, exert oneself, slave (away); keep at it, put one's nose to the grindstone; informal slog (away), plug away, put one's back into it, knock oneself out, sweat blood

While the definitions of "work" were factually accurate, it was the synonyms that struck us—words like *toil, drudgery, grind,* and *slog* were used—none of which paint a pretty picture. Is it any wonder the "Monday morning blues" or "Thank goodness it's Friday!" slogans resonate for so many of us?

As we saw in the opening stories, work is no longer the aspirational 9-to-5 office-bound activity of yesteryear. In today's world, work can happen anytime, anyplace, and with anyone. The lines between work time and personal time are blurred. It's no longer a question of work-life balance and trying to fit everything else around a standard workday. Rather, the evolving expectation is that work and life are a braided system, blended, overlapping, and seamless.

WORK IN THE FUTURE-PAST

What happened to our youthful, idealistic hopes for our future dream jobs? Did we imagine a world where we were slaves to our always-on devices or a lifestyle that allowed us to enjoy our careers?

We're at a crossroads. Will we use technology to create more freedom and success or a more oppressive relationship with work? We now have the power to choose.

The key to future-proofing both your own social time and the work that needs to be done is providing the resources that allow for both work and play. To ensure the temptation to always check e-mail is reduced, managers must face reality and allow fun, spontaneity, and other life experiences to occur.

Before you write us, please understand we're not suggesting that work can't be fun. What we *are* saying is we need to balance all the facets that make up a well-rounded life experience, including work, family, friends, and alone time. To have one facet at the cost of another means that ultimately we all suffer.

We have come full circle. If we travel back 200 years to a time before the industrial revolution that brought about the modern workplace, we would find a freelance economy where work was a 24/7 endeavor. Weekends are a relatively modern invention. In fact, the very word "freelance" is from medieval times when knights, who had not pledged loyalty to one family, were available to fight, whether in tournaments or in battle, for those willing to pay for their services—the ultimate freelancers.

In the years leading up to the industrial revolution, freelance was the basis for many jobs. During this time, people worked for themselves or in small family groups, usually out of their homes or in a nearby location. The blacksmith, the weaver, the butcher, the baker, and the candlestick maker were the industries of their day. People's relationship with work was fluid and integrated into their lifestyle.

The Industrial Revolution brought about automation that centralized production, brought the individual worker out of the weaving loft into the factory, and brought the farm workers to the burgeoning towns to seek a new type of employment. The hired hands.

These times were not all idyllic and painless. There were riots, there was resistance, and there were even organized protests. Luddites were real people, textile workers who saw the newfangled factories and massive looms as a threat to their existence and way of life. But it's safe to say the stress-management industry we know today was not yet in existence.

Technology was transforming a previously skilled industry into one where a lesser skilled (and lesser paid) labor force could deliver the same results. The Luddites of today may not be smashing equipment with hammers or throwing clogs into the machinery, but their concerns are very real. Warnings of driverless cars and advances in artificial intelligence fuel a new fear, a fear of the unknown impact on how we interact as human beings.

The factory approach has informed many of the approaches to work, management, and education that we see today. The rapid acceleration of new technologies has a direct impact on how and where work is done, and it is having a transformational impact on work that far surpasses the impact of the Industrial Revolution. We are now in the midst of the digital revolution.

In hindsight, while transformative, the Industrial Revolution was more of a gradual evolution. The rate of change was steady, and it sometimes took years to move from a concept to a design. Change happened at a local level and from there moved outward to neighboring communities, industries, and other countries.

Contrast that with the launch of Pokémon Go, from zero to 1 million-plus subscribers in less than 24 hours.

CAREER LATTICE

It's not just technology that's imposing this change on how and where work happens. It's also a shift in expectations. The

Millennial generation, born after 1980, and the upcoming Generation Z, born in the late '90s, know nothing but the technological age. They demand a more flexible work environment and are less willing to work a standard 9-to-5 schedule. Instead, they are drawn to opportunities where they can work when inspiration strikes them—as long as expectations are met and results are delivered. In the past it was about the hired hands and mind. Now it's the hired mind and heart!

They are the generation for whom the option to telecommute is not a perk or a luxury. For this upcoming generation it's the norm and the expectation. They will be the ultimate flexible workforce. Millennials have been raised on next-day or same-day delivery, and everything on demand. Work is no different for them. Sitting in rush hour traffic for two hours or catching a train to the office is anathema to this generation—a complete waste of time—instead they want to work on demand, anytime, anyplace, anywhere, and they expect bigger challenges and new career opportunities on demand, too.

The traditional career ladder is no more. The idea that if you pay your dues and stay with a company long enough, you will move up the career ladder is a fable. With the flattening of organizations the career ladder is more of a career lattice—where success isn't only about vertical movement. Success is about the horizontal opportunities that provide new experiences and expand skills.

Morag's career is a case in point: currently in her fifth career, she began as an aspiring engineer, became a corporate banker, moved into leadership development, and became a solopreneur, then an entrepreneur with a growing team, and now an author and professional speaker.

Linda's career was very much the same, moving from administrator; to union representative to the public sector;

management development; then on to finance; leadership development; and now consultant, coach, speaker, and radio show host.

Careers today don't follow nice tidy paths. They zig and they zag in response to the doors that open and opportunities that are seized.

Josh Bersin of Bersin by Deloitte recently told us, "I think there's basically a redefinition of what business is, that it isn't a hierarchical company anymore. It's a network and that is having profound implications on how we manage people, people's careers, how we develop people, and how we do performance management. All of that traditional HR stuff is getting questioned because it doesn't serve you as well in this new world. I hear this all of the time now from companies of all sizes."

He went on to describe business as "networks of people coming together for specific purposes or to solve specific, particular problems. They may work together for a couple of years. They may disband, and they may reconnect in other kinds of configurations."

The career lattice is also indicative of how the corporate hierarchy is shifting from defined hard-line reporting and top-down structure to one that is matrixed. A team member could be hard lined to one manager while dotted lined to another manager or team. We now work in a series of interconnected and interdependent networks, even if they are difficult to chart.

When we pause to consider who our bosses are, most of us will identify an ever-extending and convoluted group that includes customers, colleagues, our immediate boss, our boss' boss, the area manager, the regional leader, and the functional leader.

Learning to manage what may become competing perspectives and opinions will differentiate the high performer of the future. To future-proof your career you need to be connected at multiple levels, to multiple people, and actively cultivate those connections.

RELATIONSHIP WITH EMPLOYER

The twentieth-century expectation of work was that we provide our skills, mental and physical, to one employer in return for getting paid at a regular and predictable cadence. This forms the basis for what was described as the "psychological contract," the implicit expectations that employers had of their employees—and vice versa.

During our leadership studies in the late 1980s, we were taught that the psychological contract went something like this: Employees committed to working at a company, providing loyalty and a consistent work effort. In return, the company took care of the employee, providing pay and benefits that would last a lifetime.

For our grandfathers, a job for life was the expectation, and, in many cases, the norm. When they retired, they received pensions. For our fathers, the presumption was to join an industry and possibly move to different organizations within that industry once or twice during a career. The pension was no longer a guarantee based on their final salary; it was now determined by the value of the pension fund and the contributions made.

The idea of an employer taking care of their employees from day one through retirement seemed too good to be true then, and it's certainly too good to be true now. The rules of the employer-employee contract, whether implicit or explicit, are being rewritten for the twenty-first century.

There has been a shift from the paternalistic employer to the self-sufficient employee and from employee for life to the more flexible workforce. In the modern world, working for several employers as part-time and contract workers will continue to increase. Company pension plans are becoming less common with individual retirement accounts and stakeholder pensions becoming the responsibility of each individual.

Loyalties are shifting from the company to the team and sometimes the manager one works with. The quality of the working relationships with boss and colleagues is a key driver for staying with or leaving an employer. The Kelly Global Workforce Index 2013[3] surveyed 120,000 respondents from 31 countries across the Americas; Europe, Middle East, and Africa; and Asia Pacific. Sixty-three percent of the participants stated that the quality of the relationship with their direct manager impacted their level of satisfaction with their job.

The psychological contract is no more. Welcome to the social contract.

Relationships matter, and the quality of our working relationships matters even more in the modern world. Our willingness to tolerate toxic behaviors—the team member who takes credit for our work, the boss who yells, or being excluded from team meetings—is diminishing. Our options to seek opportunities elsewhere are endless. When people move to a new job, it's not just about the money being offered, it's also about the quality of the team experience.

The impact of globalization is changing the nature of work. No longer are individual employees competing in a local market for the next opportunity; instead we are all part of the global talent pool. The rush to outsource in the 1990s demonstrated how quickly change can occur and how new sources of talent can be tapped.

When it comes to finding new sources of talent, it seems that twenty-first-century companies are destined to play a never-ending game of global whack-a-mole. As fast as a new talent hotspot pops up, whether it's a city or a country, other companies quickly follow—draining the market for talent and extending the game as companies rush off to anticipate and capture the next talent hotspot.

Fiverr.com, Upwork.com, and TaskRabbit.com are platforms connecting a global army of freelancers with opportunities that match their skills. Tapping into the flexible economy will allow companies to scale up and down rapidly in response to market and project needs.

Transparency and opportunity on the Internet means we are now competing with an unseen colleague who may be thousands of miles and many time zones away. When you're sleeping, they're working.

Dan Pink, best-selling author of books on the changing world of work, observes "talented people need organizations less than organizations need talented people." The future of work is less of a chore or a place we have to go to. Instead, work becomes something we choose to do because we want to.

RELATIONSHIP WITH COLLEAGUES

In today's hyperconnected world it's becoming increasingly difficult to differentiate between friends and colleagues.

We spend more than 40 percent of our time with work colleagues who were strangers initially. In twentieth-century models coworkers bonded together in the same place. They built tribal relationships and often did not play well with the other tribes in the workplace. Sales competed with operations, finance competed with HR. It was politics, silos, and turf wars, with infighting tribe by tribe.

From studying the brain we know that our instinct is to put up defenses with people we don't know—unless, of course, they seem like us and then a quick bond develops. But in today's entrepreneurial global workplace this tribal attitude cannot survive. Building relationships and connections quickly, and paying attention to how we bond so that everyone is included, is paramount.

Increasingly, the workplace consists of the traditional employee, as well as contractors and independent consultants. What's uncommon is the focus on how the individual contractors and consultants are integrated into the traditional team and how they are treated.

In many organizations independent workers are still kept at arm's length. Training, social events, and access to information are usually unavailable to the flexible worker. The result is a segment of have-nots and therefore potential will-nots.

In many cases this differentiation is understandable. A legal line has be drawn to prevent the independent worker from gaining access to benefits and perks offered to full-time employees such as stock options, overtime pay, 401k accounts, and health care—in addition to matters of trade secrets, training, and confidentiality.

Deloitte's "2016 Global Human Capital Trends" report stated that contingent, contract, and part-time workers make up almost one-third of the workforce, yet many companies lack the HR practices, culture, or leadership support to manage this new workforce.

With more than 40 percent of the workforce likely to be composed of independent workers by 2020,[4] it's apparent that legislation will need to move quickly in order to keep up. In the book, *The Alliance*, Reid Hoffman (cofounder of LinkedIn), shares his vision for the future of work. The days of the career for life are gone, replaced by the concept of "tours of duty" where the nature of work is becoming more fluid and where individuals with specific skills are hired to complete a specific project.

Building alliances is essential from Reid's perspective. Employees may only work with you for a certain project cycle and then move on to another tour. They may or may not stay with your company if the mutual alliance no longer makes sense. But keeping the relationship regardless of where the person goes is essential.

Who you know and what you know is much more important than the formal role you play.

RELATIONSHIP WITH CULTURES

We are all global workers, whether we recognize that today or not.

Linda and Morag have worked with leaders on five continents and in more than 30 countries; we've seen the future.

And as globalization accelerates, the need to collaborate with colleagues from across the world increases. With globalization comes the importance of respecting cultural differences and being curious about the expectations of others. In doing so, we create respect for different approaches to how work gets done in different countries.

Working globally is no longer an opportunity afforded to just a few expatriate assignments. We are all global citizens and need to build global relationships in order to succeed.

Connecting with our colleagues is vital, whether we're sitting in an office, a cubicle, a coffee shop, or on our sofa. Our assumptions of working relationships need to change from an individualistic approach, which fueled unhealthy internal competition, to an ally mind-set, which Morag wrote about extensively in her book, *Cultivate: The Power of Working Relationships*.

As humans, we are naturally social creatures, which means the opportunity to chat with a colleague at the water cooler or stick our head in someone's office and say "hi" actually matters to a company's success.

It's no surprise that one of the key questions in Gallup's engagement research is "Do I have a best friend at work?" Effective professional relationships are not just a nice to have, they are a need to have. There is a clear correlation between a positive answer to this question and higher employee engagement, productivity, and retention.

RELATIONSHIP WITH THE COMMUNITY

The importance of the relationship between companies and the local communities in which they operate has often been overlooked, with a few notable exceptions like the garden cities in the United Kingdom and the original Industrial Revolution Quaker factories Cadbury and Clarks, to name but two. In these cases, the companies provided not just a positive working environment but also sought to have a positive impact on the family and social lives of their employees.[5]

How times have changed. Now the impact of organizations on the communities and environment around them is scrutinized.

Corporate philanthropy and corporate social responsibility (CSR) programs are a business priority and integrated into corporate strategy for many organizations. It's been said that bad news travels faster than good news. Technology has only increased the transparency of these relationships, with negative stories being published around the world in minutes.

Fair trade, clean water, environmental sustainability, local sourcing, and zero waste are initiatives on the mind of every future-thinking leader—and employee. While some CEOs might have disparaged these ideas years ago, today no one doubts the importance of community-mindedness to a brand. Additionally, these considerations are key to the relationship a company has with its community, its employees, and vendor partners.

There is a move in the European Union[6] to make a require-ment for publicly traded companies to report their CSR programs and social impact. More and more we are hearing that customers are choosing to do business with organizations that can demonstrate a positive relationship with the communities in which they operate.

CSR is one opportunity that provides employees the oppor-tunity to feel connected to something bigger than themselves and see their company supporting the social good.

Social networking happens between companies and commu-nities and goes way beyond Facebook likes. The key is to be proactive and own the message.

RELATIONSHIP WITH OUR NETWORK

Collecting "likes" and random connections is not networking. While worn as a badge of honor, simply having a large number of connections is not the same as having an effective network.

It's the quality of the connections that matters, not the quantity.

Lynda Gratton, a professor at London Business School, says this brilliantly: In the future we will all need to "stand out from the crowd while at the same time being part of the crowd or, at least, the wise crowd."[7]

She goes on to describe a future where we will all need to be able to stand out with mastery and skills while simultaneously becoming part of a collection of other masters who, together, create value. A failure to do so will likely result in us being on our own, isolated and competing with thousands of others with no possibility of leveraging what a crowd brings.

In the past, success was achieved through personal drive, ambition, and competition. In the future, success will be achieved through the subtle but high-value combination of mastery *and* connectivity. The defining factors will be what you know, who you know, and how well you can work with others.

There are now seven billion mobile devices on earth,[8] almost one for each person. Online connectivity has been jokingly referred to as the new minimum level of Maslow's hierarchy of needs.

At the time of this writing, we the authors had a combined LinkedIn network of over 6,000 people. These are first-degree connections and include people we have worked with, met at events, and partnered with—people who would take our calls. Our second-degree connections, or friends of friends, expands our network exponentially. This number doesn't include our LinkedIn followers, our Twitter followers, Facebook friends, or ScoopIt followers.

Having a network is not the same as networking. Having a network is passive, reactive, and refers to the people we are connected to through our professional work, associations, and family. Networking is proactive; it is how we use our network and web of connections to leverage our reputation, impact, and achieve our personal goals. Networking focuses on connecting with the people who can help you succeed today and help make your future goals a reality.

Forget the six degrees of separation. In the twenty-first century it's more like two degrees of connection.

However, these virtual connections are only of use if we are proactive in nurturing the relationships. As we move to a more fluid definition of work, career connections with allies become even more important—especially the "loose" connections to friends of friends.

You must intentionally connect or risk becoming disconnected. Within this second tier of connections there are opportunities that may be crucial to your future work.

In the new work order recruiting is both digital and social, personal and impersonal. It's not only who we know that's important, it's who knows *us* and who can find us that will be a key determinant of our success.

BALANCING IS NO ACT

In the future, and more important, today, we need to be even more diligent in balancing the needs of the relationships we have with work and the relationships we have with others.

Increased connectivity means we can share work and simplify our approaches. The relationships we build with others are how we avoid becoming isolated, fragmented, and—at worst—obsolete.

Most of all, we must recognize that we have no excuse for not enjoying the kind of working relationships we aspire to.

Future-Proof Your Company

- Have you relied on technology and gimmickry instead of nurturing personal relationships? How can you help employees shift from the traditional work mind-set, to embrace a digital mind-set that will impact how they manage, organize, and lead change?

- What are the digital platforms, applications, and software needed to support clearer communication across the organization?

- Have you taken a critical look at your people policies and practices to see which are helping to build relationships and which are continuing to maintain the tribal "them and us" attitudes of the past?

FUTURE-PROOF YOUR CAREER

- As you consider the tasks you're working on right now, how can you take a more relationship-oriented approach to your work?

- What workplace relationships are stressing you? What proactive steps can you take to improve those relationships?

- Take an honest look at your connections and collaborative skills. What can you do to improve those relationships?

CHAPTER **6**

Diversity and Inclusion

Future Inclusion

There are biases—some conscious and
unconscious—that have to be rooted out.
—President Barack Obama

Did you know that in the 1960s the population of the United
States was 90 percent white? For those of us who were alive
then and those who are Caucasian, that's the context in which we
were brought up.

Our tribe was white, but that didn't mean that everyone got
along and that there was no prejudice. Remember all the now
politically incorrect jokes that circulated during the '60s, '70s, and
'80s? It was okay to tell Polish jokes and pick on other ethnic
groups. Racial jokes were rampant.

Groups were excluded just because they were from different
countries or practiced difference religions that were not mainstream. It's not that the country was not diverse—it was, but it was
white diversity. Exclusionary behavior toward certain groups was
a daily occurance.

Many of us have grown up with stereotypes and an aversion
to people who are different from us. These were sometimes subtle
differences, often not rooted in obvious physical differences.

Sometimes they were differences of thought, values, behaviors, and how we lived our lives. They existed nonetheless. By virtue of being human we are exclusionary, prejudiced, and biased toward our own preferences and ways of life.

A common lament went something like this, "As a company we invested in a woman's training, then she would start having children and leave the company." The popular television show *Father Knows Best* and others like it supported the stereotype of women staying home to take care of the family and men going off to be the breadwinners. It was the more contemporary version of the primordial men are hunters and women gatherers.

SEA CHANGE

Like a fish that doesn't know it's wet, when we swim in bias long enough, we don't notice our worldview is all wet.

Prejudice, bias, and exclusionary behavior have always played a role in human society. Somehow, over time we did break down some of these deep-seated barriers, but it wasn't easy and it will never be easy. Although these older stereotypes still exist, they are not spoken about as much.

Fast-forward and now the population of the United States is trending 35 to 40 percent people of non-white races. This is a staggering increase in just 50 years and a trend that is going to continue.

This massive shift makes many uncomfortable and tests the boundaries of what we have learned about cultures, beliefs, and values. The conflict is inevitable as is the need to change.

The luxury of slow integration that existed in the past no longer exists.

Let's look at the demographics of Europe. By all accounts it has an aging population with declining birth rates. Immigrants are needed to fuel the economy. Migration of people with dramatically different cultures is happening fast with little time to digest those differences. The influx of new nationalities, religions, and race reveals a deep-seated fear—a fear that the ethnic culture of the European countries will be lost forever.

This frightens people and causes them to retreat to a safety mode—a natural mode that we now understand from studying neuroscience is deeply hard-wired in the brain.

The same reaction sometimes occurs when women invade what was traditionally male culture.

Young people today have been raised to believe they can achieve their dreams regardless of their race, gender, religion, sexual orientation, or age. But as a people we have not been able to get out of our own way in providing paths for a more inclusive society.

Have you heard this riddle?

A father and son were in a terrible car accident. The son was seriously injured, the father died. The son was rushed to the emergency room, where the doctor on call said, "I can't operate on this person because he is my son." Who was the doctor?

Most people struggle with the answer. (The doctor was the boy's mother.) Many can't solve the problem because of an unconscious bias that only men are surgeons.

THE FACTS ABOUT WOMEN

Today, many still struggle with women in leadership roles. To tackle this, Britain passed an ordinance to put more women on boards to little effect. Look around at how few minorities sit on the boards of or lead Fortune 1000 companies.

It was in 1970 when the *Wall Street Journal* coined the phrase "breaking the glass ceiling." Books were written and research was conducted to try and understand the issue. In recent decades we have only increased the number of women as CEOs of Fortune 500 companies to a little under 5 percent. Yet woman account for more than 50 percent of the global population and 46 percent of the total U.S. labor force.[1]

The picture is even bleaker for people of color. Only 0.8 percent of CEOs at Fortune 500 companies are African American and less than 2 percent are Hispanic.

Having worked in Silicon Valley leading diversity and inclusion efforts, Linda can personally attest that there were many qualified women and minorities who existed in these companies, but they were never tapped for the bigger jobs for a whole host of reasons. Many of the reasons were based on underlying beliefs that people rarely own up to.

Nobody wants to admit that they are biased toward certain people or hold beliefs that exclude others. Usually the excuses go something like this: "They lack polish, are too shy, or too assertive."

While recruiting for a senior vice president job at one of the top 10 companies in the Fortune 500, our team put together an internal slate of candidates to choose from. The slate was presented and discussed with the hiring leader and executive vice president. At this level no two candidates had exactly the same experience and credentials, but they all brought something exemplary to the table.

After much wrangling and discussion the lone woman candidate was selected. Sadly she lasted only 18 months before being forced out. She did not play poker or golf and at times had to go home to take care of her children, although she put in 12-hour days, worked weekends, and delivered results, she was perceived as contributing less than her [male] colleagues.

What some people remembered was that she had to go home to take care of her kids. Frankly, most of her male colleagues had stay-at-home wives. This woman was being consciously or unconsciously stereotyped. She just plain did not fit into the good old boys culture.

STEREOTYPING IS PERSONAL

Linda has personally experienced this type of stereotyping numerous times. At a conference, she was sitting on a dais next to her boss, and people assumed she was there as his assistant.

She was the keynote speaker.

Stereotyping is personal because we apply our own experience and intent to the situation at hand. When someone speeds past us on the highway, we tend to label them as a bad driver, a road hog, and jerk.

When we drive fast because of a family emergency or the piping hot take-out food we need to get home, we don't think of ourselves as being bad drivers, road hogs, or jerks.

We don't give others the same benefit of the doubt.

This is why forced ranking so often fails. The assumption, and bias, is that the bottom 10 percent of employees underperform. And more insidiously—will always underperform.

Inversely, executives are perceived as successful and perceive themselves as successful because they are at the senior levels rather than acknowledging their success occurred despite their flaws.

Take Susan Boyle's famous first television appearance on *Britain's Got Talent* in 2009. Despite her amazing talent and potential, she was ignored most of her life, and certainly not considered star material.[2]

As she marched onto the stage, Simon Cowell rolled his eyes, and the audience laughed.

Until she sang her first note.

How often do we overlook talent and potential because of deep-seated stereotypes and unfavorable first impressions? And how many first impressions are actually tangible examples of unconscious bias?

The 2014 Sony Pictures hacking scandal revealed that the company's female executives and producers made substantially less than their male counterparts.

We have put in place programs like day care and flexible work schedules. Quotas were established for how many women and minorities' need to be hired and promoted. Development programs offering coaching and mentoring were established for minorities to get more exposure with senior leaders. But these programs fall woefully short.

Advancement for women and minorities—and for that matter, anyone who does not fit our Western view of leaders—has been a slow trickle.

Why? Because even well-intentioned programs don't fully address unconscious bias.

WHEN BIAS SEEMS PRAGMATIC

While working with a Fortune 100 company, Linda was in charge of talent career movement. A hiring manager and she were discussing promotions for talent in his business unit with a typical conversation that went like this.

"Well, what about Jasmine for the promotion? She is a top performer, her track record with customers is excellent. Her team is the best in the department."

"She is really great but you know she has three kids and she probably won't move."

"Have you checked with her? She just might."

"No, I'm sure she won't."

Jasmine gets passed over and didn't even know it. A male counterpart, who also had three kids, was selected. The unspoken bias was that child-rearing requirements looked different for the candidates.

Jasmine ultimately left the company and started her own company. You'd be surprised how often this kind of conversation takes place behind closed doors.

Talent reviews and deciding about promotions can signal a whole host of prejudices. But the most insidious comment we've heard relates to lack of "executive presence."

Make a tally sheet and in most cases those who are perceived to lack executive presence are minorities, women, LGBTQ, introverts, and foreign nationals.

The leaders making these decisions are not necessarily bad people. They just don't realize that the subliminal messages and context they are drawing from to make decisions about others is exclusionary. We have set patterns, images, and context for what we believe people should be like, and often these are so subtle we don't even realize it.

Linda and Morag have both had mentors, male and female, who helped them along the way. Many have been staunch advocates for inclusiveness in their organizations.

One such individual is Jim Murren, chairman and CEO of MGM International, headquartered in Las Vegas, Nevada, who has mentored many women in his organization. Jim understands that diversity and inclusion is an imperative. In his hospitality and gaming business he must cater to global tourists. They make up 16 percent of the total customer base and stay twice as long as domestic travelers. In his company 45 percent of the employee base is minority and 48 percent are women.

The changing demographics of the new workforce make inclusive hiring an imperative.

Stand at the front door of any global corporation today and you will see diverse talent walk in and out in droves. But go to the executive floors and you will see a very different picture. This is the real point. The opportunity to be included at top levels of organizations is still slim.

Even after all the programs, quotas, awareness training, and pressure to put diverse talent in greater roles of authority, the speed of action has been glacial. These attitudes are by no means directed only at women and minorities. White males who want to spend more time with their families are experiencing backlash too. Many males cite not wanting to take child care leave when they have a newborn for fear it will adversely impact their career.

The question is not really about diversity but about how we ensure that those who are different are included. If you can't include others who are different, your business will not survive. We can no longer attack the symptoms. We must own up to the root cause.

> Until you make the unconscious conscious, it will
> control your life and you will call it fate.
> —*Carl Jung*

BRAIN SCIENCE, BIAS, AND DIVERSITY

We all have unconscious bias that causes us to embrace some and discriminate against others. And this distinction happens unconsciously and instantly.

The last frontier of the human body—the brain—is finally being understood in more depth. As we examine how the human brain works we begin to understand why long-held views are hard to change. We have known for some time that the brain's function is to fight anything that poses a threat to our survival.

Neuroscientists' recent research has proven conclusively that the brain's primary function is to keep us safe. It detects threats of all sorts and reacts accordingly.

The brain collects clues about what constitutes danger and then elicits a mental and physical reaction. Many times people perceived as threats are different-looking people and tribes with unfamiliar practices that endangered the survival of their own tribe. Our brains learned to be wary of others who were not like us.

This has been the cause of many wars over the centuries. We have learned not to trust people who are not like us because they have attacked us, taken our territory, or pillaged our property. These stored subliminal memories signal the brain and trigger a threat response before we even realize it.

The brain evolves in a context, and over 11,000 messages hit the brain during any given minute. These messages create synapse and internal connections that shape our reactions. For example, we see a red light and put our foot on the brake before we're even aware of it.

The brain, and the context in which it was developed, forms a kind of human gyroscope that keeps us in balance throughout the day. It enables us to be safe in most of the circumstances we encounter without having to consciously think about the situation.

Bias impacts our behavior every single moment. During a recent client visit in Mexico we were making our way to dinner. As we climbed a series of steps we were laughing and, in the next minute, Linda laid sprawled on the ground. What had happened? After we picked her up and dusted her down, we realized that the steps were not the standard height that we are used to in the United States. In fact every tread was a slightly different height to the one before. The step that tripped Linda up was higher than any other. A painful example of our internal gyroscope being thrown out of balance.

A 1980s study by Benjamin Libet found that study participants moved their finger before they were consciously aware of wanting to move their finger. This study, and other similar studies, concluded that "an unconscious part of your brain 'wills' an action before you are consciously aware of your wanting to direct" movement.

Another famous study built on Libet's findings using encephalographs to study the brains of students and how they reacted to certain signals. This research again showed that the brain initiates action before the conscious mind is aware of it.

In other words, if your brain has been conditioned to believe that males hold executive roles or that women can't do certain types of work, you will react and make a decision before you're even aware of it. You will react before you realize that you had a negative or positive response.

STEREOTYPING AND PERSONAL BELIEFS

If you study history, you see deep-seated historical and psychological distrust among various countries that still carry over today. The Eurovision Song Contest plays this out in real time, year after year. Voting for the winning song and country follows a predictable pattern that reflects millennia of rivalry and history.

The French and English have always had a cantankerous relationship. Japan and China are other good examples. The suspicions have been so engrained in these countries that it can be difficult for some to get past their dislike for each other.

The brain stores memories and emotions. It captures every story you have ever been told and categorizes it. Stories of countries in conflict and enemies are in your subconscious. These stories raise your awareness when confronted with a similar situation, and you react even when the story may no longer be applicable. This is an example of unconscious bias.

Unconscious brain function makes up approximately 80 percent of the brain's activity.

It is not that we inherently dislike other people, but we have been programmed with subliminal and not-so-subliminal messages. This includes, but is certainly not limited to, media advertising that covertly promotes an ideal figure for women, which consciously and unconsciously impacts our self-image. There are some 100 billion neurons in the brain, and each is connected to many others, creating a network of connections. These shape our values and ultimately shape how we each respond to life's situations.

VICIOUS CYCLES

A young girl grew up in South Philadelphia where she was told that Italians who lived on the next block were not to be trusted. Her parents believed they were mafia because that is what their parents were told about Italians.

This little girl grew up to have a very negative bias toward Italians that still lingers today and impacts the stories she tells her own children. Three generations of one family impacted by bias.

Another interesting study of the brain revealed some startling facts regarding empathy. When people were asked about feelings for someone who was injured, they professed to have empathy. Certain portions of their brains would glow on the screen showing strong empathy for the injured individual.

When they were shown injured people of a different race, they would again *say* they were empathetic to their plight. But their brains' responses were not as intense and glowed less than if the person was of the same background or race. The researchers concluded that despite our professed feelings, many find it harder to identify with others' plights if they are different from us.

We all have bias. Some gets in the way of personal growth and societal progress. This is the root cause of why programs and processes to increase diversity in the workplace have not worked and will not work—until we come to grips with our own unconscious bias.

BIAS IN THE MIRROR

Another factor revealed by studying the brain is that the messages sent to us as children carry over into adulthood.

Some children grow up being told they can't do certain jobs, can't play certain sports, or are not smart. These messages impact their view of themselves and the perceived capabilities. If people think they're not smart or can't do something, it impacts their behavior, their values, and how they live their lives.

A recent news story highlights this. An elementary school teacher asked the class to draw pictures of fighter-pilots, surgeons, and fire fighters. Of the 60-plus drawings, less than a handful showed women in these roles. Bias is formed early.

Parents unwittingly pass on their bias and stereotypes to their children causing an unconscious reaction in their children that can either help them or hinder them as they move into society. This is one explanation for a current phenomenon among women shown in recent research.

Many women don't aspire to the most senior roles, despite the fact that more women have advanced degrees than ever before. They were conditioned to believe they could not attain those jobs. The unconscious message that played in their heads was they could only get so far in an organization.

We've interviewed many such women with outstanding credentials who just don't believe that having a top role is achievable. Many also believe they can't do that role without a great deal of personal and family sacrifice. The messages they were sent as children is that certain levels of success are beyond their reach.

Other women were told they could do anything, believed that, and acted accordingly. These are the women who broke through the barriers.

In Linda's recent interview with *Inc.* magazine's editor-in-chief, Eric Schurenberg, he said, "if you live in a culture in which it's accepted that members of your group perform worse at a particular exercise than the population at large, then if you're given that task and reminded of this societal prejudice, you will do worse than the average group that hasn't been reminded of this supposed disability."

REWIRING INCLUSION

The good news is that the brain can rewire with repetition.

Since childhood, a young man was told that he was not athletic and could not catch a ball. He was participating in a research-based learning experience where he was told that he would have to catch an orange. The man responded that he wasn't good at catching.

The trainer then showed the man the orange and asked him to concentrate on the navel of the orange. He then tossed the man the orange, and he caught it without dropping it. He repeated the exercise several times, and the man continued to catch the orange. He was rewiring his brain from a negative stereotype he learned in his youth.

The trainer then tossed him a ball the next time and told him to focus on the color of the ball. The man was again successful.

All your neurons, circuitry, and synapses can respond differently if you can rewire your thinking. If you grew up like most of us did, you were constantly being told, "Don't do this and don't do that." Yet annoyingly, you continued to do those things. "Don't suck your thumb" doesn't work. This approach of telling people what not to do is totally counter to how the brain learns.

Scientists now know that telling someone not to do something generates a picture in their mind of them doing something.

Therefore, that is exactly what they do. Reframing the picture to something positive changes the dynamic. Instead of saying "don't wet the bed," a better way to achieve the result is to say, "Picture yourself sleeping through the night in a nice, dry bed."

We see these kinds of triggers on the golf course all the time. A cart partner will say, "Don't hit into the water on the left." Invariably most golfers in the foursome hit into the water. Instead, envision yourself hitting the ball straight down the fairway. Every time you do this you'll hit a great shot (including occasional great shots into the water).

TAKING ACTION

The action we all must take is to dump the focus on diversity and all the programs devoted to shaming and blaming others for lack of diversity.

The word diversity has become too closely associated with the failed focus on "don't." Instead, let's focus on inclusion as the positive, and more accurate, alternative.

Understand that we are already diverse in so many ways. It has always been part of what makes us human and who we are.

Creating a culture that fully embraces, and includes, all participants is essential for a future-proof organization.

Inclusion is the new paradigm that replaces the old paradigm of diversity. And the first step is honesty.

FUTURE-PROOF YOUR COMPANY

- Leaders often delegate inclusiveness to HR. Realize that everyone in every department must own company culture. The next time you're hiring or promoting and can't find anyone who's any good stop and consider if bias is involved.

- Take practical steps to acknowledge bias. There are many tools and techniques to do this. One in particular is the Implicit Association Test developed by Harvard. Bias does not make us good or bad, but it does sometimes get in the way of what we ultimately say we want to do and be.

- Pull groups of leaders and employees together and paint a picture of what a truly inclusive workplace looks like. What are people doing, how are they treating each other, what are the rules of the road for inclusion? Use this picture to help others reshape and rewire their brains to celebrate others. Then examine your workplace practices to see if and how they support or limit this positive picture of inclusion.

- The real danger is settling for platitudes over real change.

FUTURE-PROOF YOUR CAREER

- Make sure you aren't modeling what you're fighting against. "Inclusiveness begins with me." Look for opportunities to help people to talk about tough issues in a respectful way.

- Understand your triggers. What exactly tips your bias to the forefront of your brain and drives you to unconscious action? This is an excellent way to bring the unconscious bias to the conscious level.

- Rewire your brain. Paint a positive picture of how you will respond, and respond that way until it becomes a habit. Find someone who is different from you who you would normally not talk to and spend some time asking him what is most important to him about his work and about his family. See how much common ground you really have.

- Check the mirror for unconscious bias against yourself. What negative stereotypes and limitations have you allowed to be imposed on yourself? Then take steps to rewire your brain.

CHAPTER 7

Technology

Resistance Is Futile

> Resistance is futile. You will be assimilated.
> —The Borg Collective

C ould we run a business without Post-it notes? Perhaps.

But can anyone run a business, or a career, without technology? Not a chance. The time for us to opt out, or use it selectively, is long past. Technology is ever present, ever advancing, and ever pernicious.

We are firmly in the embrace of the fourth industrial revolution, a digital revolution that impacts every aspect of our lives—at work, at play, and at home.

The boundaries between historically diverse disciplines, health care and IT, for example, have become increasing blurred and intertwined. It's almost a chicken and egg situation, prompting the question, *which came first—the technology or the intertwining?*

When Morag and Linda entered the twentieth-century workforce, their bosses were down the hall. Now the boss is often in a different city or another country.

In the past, if you wanted an answer to a medical question, you consulted a local expert or a textbook. Now you can look at a hologram image of a patient while consulting with an expert in another country.

Technology will continue to both disrupt industries and create new opportunities. You can be a casualty of the disruption or reap the benefits of applied innovation. It's your choice.

Be clear: no job, no company, and no industry is immune from the impact of technology.

Look at the publishing industry as one example of technological change. The early impact of Internet technology was in the newspaper industry. Soon, e-book technologies began to disrupt the book world, including brick-and-mortar retailers. But at the same time, the world of publishing was opened up to millions of new authors—and new readers.

Are you reading a print copy of this book or an e-book? The irony is not lost on us! We see a time when, once again, traditionally printed books will be seen as a luxury item and certain publications will be esteemed as a status symbol. This trend comes full circle from when the printing press was first invented and only the rich could afford to purchase books.

Now publishers and indie authors offer free books just to generate leads and marketing data. With digitization publishers know your every reading habit, which genres you like, what time you read, and data is being captured every moment. Amazon even knows how many pages you've read on the Kindle version.

Technology has transformed the retail industry. Brick-and-mortar stores are no longer the priority for consumers. Online retail puts almost any item within reach of customers who don't need to live close to shopping centers, transforming our buying habits.

When was the last time you made a major purchase without going online first to compare options?

We research online, we go to the big box store to touch and try the product, then return home to complete the purchase online. The next wave of the retail experience is nearly upon us. With AmazonGo we can literally walk into the store, pick up what we want, with payment happening automatically without the need for cash or credit card. The ultimate in convenience.

Just wait until your home is also a manufacturing plant.

3-D printing is producing solutions as diverse as rocket parts, artificial limbs, rapid prototypes, and even food. NASA has been quoted as saying 3-D printed rocket parts are as durable as those created through traditional manufacturing processes—but 70 percent less expensive.[1] NASA recently e-mailed the design of a part to the International Space Station and it was "printed on site." Same day delivery but without the shipping costs!

TECHNOLOGY THE DISRUPTER AND ENABLER

The ever-increasing pace of change in technology and innovation is breathtaking. What we viewed with awe and wonder a few years ago is considered humdrum and ordinary today. Science fiction is becoming science fact every minute.

The ideas and technology that currently feel far-fetched or too expensive will become mainstream in a matter of years or even months.

You only have to recall the brick-sized mobile phones or remember family members asking, "why would I need a mobile phone?" to see how quickly we have learned to adapt and adopt technology.

New technology may require considerable investment to create the first-to-market solution, but it is lowering the barriers to entry for those who follow. Technology isn't just providing existing services in new ways, it's connecting what were disparate processes to provide an even more seamless and pleasant customer experience.

Airbnb connects those who travel and need a place to stay with people who have rooms or homes to rent out. It is disrupting the hotel and travel industry. Airbnb has more bedrooms available than the largest global hotel chains—and yet employs fewer than 1,000 staff members, without owning any property.

Technology has transformed the publishing industry. Want to write a book (and apparently there is a book inside each of us)? You can self-publish in a matter of hours.

Technology is not only disrupting what is created and delivered to consumers, it's also disrupting what is captured and understood about consumers and nonconsumers.

DATA IS BIG

Digitization of information is pervasive. Even if the data is currently not being utilized or fully mined, you can bet it is being captured and stored. This data is ready for historical analysis, trend analysis, and will be used to inform future decisions.

Big data can be described as vast, growing stores of information that can be analyzed by computers to reveal trends, patterns, and associations. The most impactful use of big data relates to our behavior and relationships.

Analyzing this information is a burgeoning industry in itself. Are you alarmed when ads pop up in your browser for the exact item you were shopping for a few minutes before? Just wait until some of your actions are not just followed but *predicted*!

Forget *1984* and Big Brother. This data machine is more like your brother, sister, second cousin, and the stranger sitting next to you on the train, who all know things about you. Personal and organizational information isn't just being pulled from the Internet as our actions are tracked, but from data that we push out to the world through social media and every other technology platform.

Every time we announce our presence, when we check into the restaurant or landmark, or when we swipe left or right, we're leaving digital breadcrumbs that will be consumed by the voracious appetite of big data analysts—both legal and illegal.

This abundance of valuable information is driving the emergence of new businesses. Products and services are developed in the field of cybersecurity in order to stay one step ahead of hackers and those who have ill intent when it comes to accessing our data. It's estimated that cybercrime costs the world's consumers an eye-watering $110 billion annually.

Big data allows us to make connections and see patterns that may not have been visible to us before, much like the flights over the Nazca Desert of southern Peru in 1940 revealed man-made patterns in the topography. These famous lines were known centuries earlier but not fully appreciated until seen from thousands of feet above.

Future bird's-eye views of data will allow for new perspectives and new ways of thinking as the Internet of Things continues to expand. We will be able to analyze and model situations at both a macro and micro level—and the data will be more and more available to you and me.

Google Maps highlights traffic flow so individuals can choose a different route to work, the app actually makes intelligent selections on a micro level—most of the time, anyway. On a macro level, this fast data allows city planners to identify where to augment public transportation solutions and infrastructure.

In the twentieth century, London taxi drivers studied for two years to pass "The Knowledge"—essentially memorizing the streets of London to become a black cab driver.

Uber and Lyft obliterate this model. Almost anyone can now be a taxi driver. With GPS and map apps, you not only get from point A to point B, you can receive real-time alerts about traffic issues. Memorizing the streets of London is no longer necessary. We are becoming both empowered by and dependent on data and automation; memorization is a dying art. How many phone numbers do you know from memory (other than your own)?

Before you get too complacent, the disruption created by Uber and the potential to be a taxi driver is already becoming obsolete. Millions of professional drivers could be replaced by driverless cars in the next few decades. And these new driverless cars will send and receive data every mile. What is new and transformational today can be old and obsolete tomorrow. At least you and I will be able to text and ride as our cars chauffeur us to our next destination.

Fast data will impact business in the next 10 years like fast-food has impacted waistlines.

Genuine Intelligence

Data gathering is one thing, but we haven't even scratched the surface for artificial intelligence (AI) and the strides being made in the field of robotics.

Algorithms are becoming more complex and engineering solutions are being shrunk to nanotechnology as these disciplines continue to converge. What will be the impact on the processes and services your company utilizes and provides?

As the Borg ominously declared in *Star Trek: The Next Generation* television series, "Resistance is futile, you will be assimilated."

But no need to panic. Yet. While IBM's Deep Blue may play a mean game of chess, and its Watson supercomputer is beating contestants on *Jeopardy* writing pop music and movie trailers, they can't yet replace the whole human psyche. Humans had to apply the sound and music to the movie trailer. These devices can't respond, in the moment, to all the subtle nuances of language or intent. Right, Hal?

Yet AI is already here, driving our cars, providing real-time translation services, reducing language barriers, and providing new delivery mechanisms through drones and virtual assistant services like Google Home, Alexa, Cortana, and Siri.

Technology innovation isn't just about the future and creating the new. It's also having a jarring impact on traditional businesses and careers. We are seeing the seeds of change in accountancy with apps and software changing the role of CPA firms, insurance companies with online portals handling complex quotations in nanoseconds, and the legal profession with interactive online tools creating robust documents without human interaction.

For every market pressure technology provides, a new market opportunity emerges. Capitalizing on these business opportunities and making the difficult choices required for change are uniquely human capabilities.

Whether artificial intelligence and robotics will eventually replace jobs is an ongoing debate. The industrial revolution showed that some work and jobs as we currently know them will disappear, with new roles and work being created.

This was the concern of the Luddites. And history has proven that the Luddites were wrong—in the long term. One opportunity goes away and another replaces it.

It would seem to us that AI and robotics can only create long-term value if the new processes, systems, and apps *augment* the economic system as it currently operates.

Economies, whether local, national, or global, operate by allowing the transfer of value (money) from one person to another, connecting the producer with the consumer through the efforts of the employer and employee. Employees earn a paycheck that they can then spend (or invest) as consumers, transferring value back to the producer and employer. So the cycle continues.

Remove any of these players, for example, replace the employee with a robot, and the cycle is potentially broken, unless that employee is able to earn a paycheck in a new role. The time-saving and cost-savings that automation provides is a short-term benefit if the long-term impact of less employment (and, hence, less money to spend) is not considered.

There are invisible and unintended consequences of these decisions.

Ironically, the more technology and software impacts our world, the more important true soft skills become. It's not just the digital interface that businesses needs to focus on, or that rules the day. The human interface also matters. The careers, and companies, that stay focused on the human benefits of technology will live long and prosper.

UPLOADING INTO SOCIETY

Technology isn't just rewriting how business gets done, it's rewiring how society happens, what privacy means, and who owns the data being collected. Governments are scrambling to understand the impact of technology and rewrite laws and rules designed for past centuries. Those rules simply no longer apply.

This isn't a thesis on the dark side of digitization and technological advancements, nor is it a prediction about when we'll upload our consciousness into a robotic host. Personally, I wouldn't wish that on my temperamental vacuum cleaner, but times change.

But let's go into the future with our eyes wide open; there are always unintended consequences that result from change.

Morag recalled when the U.K. bank branch she worked at years ago had its first fax machine delivered. The staff thought they had finally reached the modern world. Yet within a few short years the fax machine, along with the pager, came to represent an obsolete technology.

We don't recall the last time we sent a fax, and it always amazes us how many people still have fax numbers on their business cards.

When e-mail was first introduced to workplaces, management's concern was that employees would send confidential data outside of their organization.

With a few notable (and some laudable) cases of whistle-blowing, this did not occur. E-mail became the de facto communication method, threatening snail mail and traditional handwritten notes. Postal services around the world are still struggling to reinvent themselves, to remain relevant in an ever-declining paper-based world.

However, despite the rapid rise of e-mail, the millennial generation does not use this as a primary communication tool; instead it is an identity tool, since every app and every site one joins requires an e-mail address as the primary identifier or user name.

The days of e-mail as a primary business communication tool are numbered as it is being replaced by instant messaging, Google Hangouts, Slack, and other project management tools.

The initial focus of mechanical technology seemed to be on cost-saving and productivity improvements. In stark terms, the goal was less human interaction. The immediate impact was on automation and the blue-collar workforce. Production times were slashed from months to days, along with error rates and rework.

New paradigms and tools such as Lean Six Sigma emerged. Roles changed as robots automated the assembly line and changed the need for, and nature of, physical work.

The current—and future—focus will be on augmenting or replacing humans in virtually all areas of our lives—at home, at work, and at play. Robots will impact not just the physical work required but the mental work required.

Remember that in the marketplace, scarcity drives value. If your career or business model can be replicated by a growing number of people and machines, your value goes down.

Every day, every minute, there's a new competitor entering your market, and new competitors eyeing your career. The impact of information technology will be felt across all areas of business, especially in white-collar roles. No one can escape.

Technology will redefine the expectations of workers and performance management. And, hopefully, it will free us up to do the things we're gifted in and enjoy!

WHAT'S YOUR RESPONSE TIME?

Some 3,083 e-mails arrived in Morag's inbox last month.

No wonder she feels busy all day—especially with her manic read-action-delete approach. We doubt she is alone in this dilemma. We can almost see you shaking your head along with us.

This is an example of not adapting to technology. After all, we don't rush to open every snail-mail letter that arrives—except on our birthdays. The danger for us all, and our businesses, is operating in the twenty-first century with twentieth-century mind-sets, work habits, and rules that no longer apply.

We're not predicting exactly which technologies will emerge. By the time this book was released from the publisher, companies and technologies may have already been replaced. But we are predicting that if you and your teams don't stop resisting technology, you'll be left behind.

Like it or not, people work in small chunks of time, not huge blocks. Technology is driving byte-sized attention spans. Maybe we need to adjust our workdays from the 9-to-5 all-you-can-eat buffet at your desk to the in-the-moment rapid response that's integrated throughout the day.

As with any revolution, it's not just what's going away that will have the biggest impact on us, it's what will be created and utilized in its place. The bigger question is, how do we anticipate, adapt, and respond to what's new while recognizing which technologies are staying?

We still need health care, education, construction, and food production. How we meet these needs, and how we contribute our unique value to the systems used to deliver these services, will change.

The financing business has changed. With the emergence of crowdsourcing and microfunding, businesses that did not have access to capital are now able to flourish.

It's the Internet and access to digital data that empowers a freelance economy, allowing companies of all sizes access to resources and expertise they don't have and have no intention of bringing in-house. This allows freelance businesses to focus on their unique value and core competence.

In 2010, Procter & Gamble sourced more than 50 percent of innovation externally through an open innovation program called Connect+Develop. That compares to less than 10 percent in 2001.[2]

> The new competition is not about internal knowledge
> and focus, but rather about an organization's ability to
> reach out, partner, and develop outside relationships
> and subsequent products based on these relationships.
> —*Chris Thoen, former head of Procter & Gamble's
> Open Innovation*

The Industrial Revolution was the result of new power sources. The mechanical revolution brought about standardization in parts, in processes, and in skills, replacing many of the individual craftsmen and cottage industries such as weavers, blacksmiths, matchmakers, and home workers.

Digital transformation impacts what we know and how we analyze data. This allows for increased flexibility, not standardization.

For example, companies like Vistaprint and StickerGiant have printing equipment that can switch between designs as fast as the digital input changes. These real-time technological adjustments allow companies to adapt and respond faster and more efficiently to customer demands.

How fast can you and your company adapt?

In the pharmaceutical industry, the introduction of personalized pharmacy creates drug formulas adapted to reflect the unique DNA and needs of the patient. Medicine is no longer a one-size-fits-all proposition.

Legislators usually create sweeping laws and detailed regulations in reaction to problems. But they often overlegislate and complicate in the process. Corporations do the same thing, which we'll talk about in a future chapter.

To thrive in the midst of rapid technological change, we've got to make work simpler—not continue to add complexity. But as you may have noticed, it usually takes more energy to simplify.

FUTURE WORKFORCE

The workforce of the future is one that's iterative and agile. Rules and procedures become guidelines that inform today's process but not necessarily tomorrow's. Experience and data analytics allow for the real-time adaptation of the process.

We've seen it in IT with the move from waterfall methodologies to agile methodologies. Design and testing is inculcated throughout the development phase, not just at the beginning and end of the process. This requires informed risk taking and the courage to try and fail fast so one can learn fast and adapt.

This agile mind-set, skill set, and organizational structure with flash teams is not just the future, it's the mainstream of today. And it requires a personal and cultural embracing of new technologies.

CHANGING IDENTITIES

Technology is changing how we think, how we learn, how we behave, how we interact, and how we work.

Who doesn't love getting to the end of an Uber journey and not having to go through the cumbersome process of paying? Uber connects the driver, passenger, *and the payment process*. That's what's revolutionary, and valuable, about this transformation.

How we behave is affected by our ability to order our triple-espresso-no-foam-latte on our phones before we arrive at the coffee shop. We send birthday greetings because Facebook reminded us. For many of us, our smartphone is the first thing we look at in the morning and the last thing we look at before we fall asleep. It's glued to our hand, our eyes rarely straying from the glow of the screen and the constant bombardment of information.

Keeping up with the Joneses, across the street and across the world, shows us what success is. Advertisements follow us from screen to screen, reminding us not to forget to purchase the items we glanced at yesterday. The change is that we grow to expect these wonders at breakneck speed.

When Morag worked in banking, she spent time in the workforce planning department. It was driven by first-generation spreadsheets and manually compiled data. HR analytics are still key to future organizational success because we need to understand what attracts, retains, or causes employees to leave organizations.

Now apps fill the need. Workers are drawn from an ever-larger talent pool. The twenty-first-century company leverages technology to identify talent anywhere and gives workers the freedom to choose to work when, where, and how much they want.

Identifying factors that differentiate your high performers from your average performers allows informed intervention at a corporate level, reducing the impact of human bias. Anticipating skills gaps, changing demographics, or changing technologies is much better than dealing with unforeseen consequences of change.

Talent analytics will go beyond informing the employee life cycle and employee experience. They will directly link to, inform, and respond to the business strategy. This results in a greater chance of success for the company, for the team, and for the individual.

LinkedIn, the largest accessible database of talent and jobs, can now mine the skills that are available in a particular city and compare the skills to the jobs available. Potential job seekers can see where to best use their skills. Employers will be able to precisely target talent and schools to fill the skill gaps.

Consumers expect uninterrupted technological miracles from suppliers. But is that your expectation from your management or peers at work?

Look at the recent outcry at Apple for eliminating the headphone jack from its new iPhone 7. Without white cords connecting our ears to a device, how will we pretend to be busy when we sit next to someone we don't want to talk to?

This dynamic also speaks to the cultural implications of technology. Years ago cell phone companies were faced with legislation forcing them to plan a universal charger.[3] Organizations are still trying to protect their "secret sauce." The faster technology changes, the more proprietary technology will become a thing of the past, what was once unique becomes uniform when information becomes ubiquitous.

On-demand services like Uber and TaskRabbit require an on-demand workforce. The gig economy is our future.

For years, Upwork.com and Fiverr.com have allowed us to tap into the global talent market in seconds, adding competition and creating new opportunities at the same time.

This is the employment version of the sharing economy.

More and more, employers will tap into a flexible workforce, growing and shrinking teams at the click of a button. But the downside also looms. These freelancers can't come to meetings or social gatherings, and they can create legal complications surrounding traditional employee communications.

Future employees and freelancers will expect to fit work around life rather than life around work. The question of "who owns the work contract?" becomes a key question and demands clear answers.

The future requires critical thinking skills. Do I know the keywords to use in order to Google the information I need? Can I apply my critical thinking skills to sort fact from fiction and then apply the information successfully? Memorization, a key skill of the twentieth century, is now a less valuable skill.

Do I know which "phone-a-friend" colleague can help me resolve a problem? Just-in-time learning is going to be a critical requirement for a thriving career.

Everything Is Connected and Transparent

Glassdoor.com is driving transparency in salary and corporate culture. This thrills some and scares the daylights out of others. Welcome to the future.

If someone finds himself daydreaming about a career at some tech wonderland, he might find that every company has its own version of crazy. Getting rid of titles and organizational charts might sound great—until you have a question to ask.

Secret recipes, from fried chicken to employee retention, are a myth. There are no secrets. Thank, or curse, technology.

In your business or career, there are people using information and technology to improve on your offerings and skills. There are no boundaries. People in developing countries have access to the same information you do.

Initial expertise and first-to-market gets you a seat at the table. But keeping pace and growing keeps you there.

Years ago, NASA would have spent years cataloging photos taken by the Hubble Space Telescope[4] or any of its probes sent to the outer reaches of the galaxy. Now, much of this work is being completed by volunteers around the world who scrutinize and catalog data. The same method is being utilized for a recent translation project on the Dead Sea Scrolls and in medical studies.

Why the shift in approach? They faced reality. The challenge was too big for a traditional workforce in a traditional organization. As leaders, we have to admit that the problems we face are too big to tackle without collaboration.

And people are more than willing to participate under the right conditions. Whether it's a spare seat in the car, a spare room, or a spare hour of expertise, we have access to skilled talent around the globe.

The winners will have the best human interface.

PERSONAL IMPACT

How we structure organizations and the way we collaborate and achieve results can no longer be based on the Industrial Revolution and traditional management theories. Instead the future of work will be informed by insights from neuroscience, game design, new expectations of work and life (not work *or* life), and what it means to be a happy, productive member of society. It's no longer about just hired hands or hired minds. The twenty-first century also requires hired hearts.

We remember watching television and being warned by our parents about getting "square eyes" if we watched too much. We didn't, but modern technology is bringing about a whole raft of health issues. Hunched over our screens, with heads tipped forward, it's been said that sitting is the new smoking.

With the never-ending flood of data and increased connection, the new risk is cognitive overload. The next shift will be to intelligent technology, which will sort through information and recommend informed decisions.

Morag has a fitness app on her phone, and it knows more about her than she cares to think about. She is not alone. On a global level, companies are collecting every bit of data they can. Someone is analyzing data from a million apps, creating conclusions about preferences and products we'll buy.

This model will soon transform every aspect of our lives, including our health care—actually predicting problems before they become life-threatening. Who hasn't looked at a medical website to try to self-diagnose an ache or pain. However, we've seen nothing yet! Companies as diverse as Apple, Google, and traditional health-care organizations are investing billions of dollars to develop biometric sensors and new technology solutions to support the patient, before we become ill! The modern day equivalent of the Star-Trek Tricorder is nearly upon us.

Apps already exist that remind patients to take their medications and allow doctors to see real-time measurements, whether blood pressure or heart rate.

The next generation of health-care technology, when combined with big data, could help prevent disease and extend lifespans. There is no doubt that we are on the cusp of a transformation in health care.

Transparency and speed of data bring to mind the metaphor of a butterfly flapping its wings in Colorado and causing a typhoon in Japan. But now the flap and effect happen in seconds, not months.

Consider the economic crash of 2008. There are many opinions as to the cause, but everyone would agree there were several interconnected catalysts, each driven by technology and instant communications. A few rogue butterflies crippled an industry and impacted millions of people.

In other words, if lemmings had social media, they'd be extinct by now.

Your Reality

Every company, including yours, is now a technology company.

Many companies say they're in health care, publishing, or manufacturing, but they overlook the impact of technology in transforming their markets. These are the companies that risk being left behind. Publishers can cling to printed books as their business or embrace the reality that first and foremost they are a digital business. Even manufacturers must be digital marketers.

Even at SkyeTeam, our service may be training and leadership development, but we must embrace technology to design those materials, reach our clients, and remain current. (Hence the need for shared ownership of technology processes and policies.)

To future-proof your company, you must first future-proof your mind-set.

In a recent conversation with an executive at a geographically dispersed health care provider, we discussed the need to lead by using new technology.

"We have Skype, but nobody is using it." Think about this in your workplace. How often do we unconsciously rely on old ways of working and collaborating?

In our experience as presenters in boardrooms around the world, nobody ever uses those electronic whiteboards. Have you? Few know how to use them, and many fear losing important information. (Yes, we still find ourselves snapping photos of these whiteboards.)

We get the smartphone but end up playing with the box it came in. We forget to videoconference (using the excuse that we don't like to see ourselves on camera), and we're missing opportunities to create more meaningful relationships through technology.

We have all the shiny objects at our disposal. Instead of restricting access, encourage a culture of playing with all the toys to connect and do great work. In the process, time will be wasted, but you'll also unlock new creativity and productivity.

Until recently, the employee experience, from hiring to firing and from onboarding to retirement, has been the primary responsibility of the personnel/HR department. And technology was owned by IT.

Or to put it bluntly, HR handles the people, and IT handles the machines. In many organizations, never the twain shall meet.

The opposite of this obsolete mind-set is the formation of flash teams,[5] skilled professionals who have probably never met before and may even work on different continents, who can come together to turn a napkin sketch into a viable product within days or weeks.

Results like this don't happen in technology silos.

HR is typically not a data-intense part of an organization, but that's all changing. Today, data can come from a variety of sources, ranging from performance numbers and attendance, to surveys and tracking employee life events. Smart HR leaders can tap data and determine exactly who will thrive in their companies and who will not.

The retirement of many baby boomers was delayed as a result of the 2008 financial crisis. Now that economies seem to be stabilizing, this group will be rapidly stepping away from the workforce. Many organizations are not prepared.

CATCHING THE WAVE

Resistance is futile . . . because whether you realize it or not, you've already been assimilated.

Moore's Law states the rate of computing power doubles every 18 months.

Srini Koushik, the CTO of Magellan Health, recently shared with us in an interview that some people argue that Moore's Law is coming to an end in a year or two. It describes linear growth; today it's all about exponential growth.

Years ago, when someone started their career at IBM, everyone was very proud of the fact that the company had 400,000 people across the globe. And that scale gave the company an advantage in the marketplace. That's not true today. When you look at Apple, they have 30,000 employees. So that linear relationship—every time a company grows, they've got to grow the infrastructure—has been broken, and this leads to a completely new paradigm.

This is key to the digital revolution we are experiencing. Are you and your organization keeping pace?

We want your company and career to thrive. Stop worrying about technology and start enjoying the benefits. Stop fixating on one piece of software or ignoring IT innovation, and explore all the emerging possibilities.

Who knows, you might just create a new technology.

Future-Proof Your Company

- What will we be taking for granted in five years?

- What are you taking for granted today?

- How can you leverage technology to augment your work and your company?

- All the data in the world won't help solve problems if employees don't know how to access, analyze, and apply the information. Use technology to fail faster and reward experimentation.

- Connect HR and IT—personally and technologically. Make sure you use technology to actually build trust and relationships. If the sense of community is declining, the speed and quality will suffer. That's one reason why most disruptive companies are brand-new, not the old guard. Eliminate the work dynamic of "I submit my piece of code, throw it over fence, and never know how my contribution was used."

FUTURE-PROOF YOUR CAREER

- Take a hard look at your entrenched work habits. Are you e-mailing when you could be videoconferencing? Are you getting work done or inspiring new levels of creativity by leveraging technology? Try new stuff with new tools. Today.

- Don't be the leader who is too old to understand or doesn't like technology. That's a lame excuse, and your colleagues know it. Find a technology mentor today.

- Pay attention to your social media and digital footprint. It matters and will be researched by potential recruiters and bosses. Ensure your online brand matches your real-world brand.

CHAPTER **8**

Learning

Curious Learners

The illiterate of the twenty-first century will not be those who cannot read and write, but those who cannot learn, unlearn, and relearn."

—Alvin Toffler

A lvin Toffler wrote his seminal book, *Future Shock*, nearly 40 years ago. In it he proposed the high pace of change would cause people to recoil and experience "future shock." Essentially he posited that too much change happening in too short a period of time overwhelms a population.

If you hope things might slow down, don't hold your breath. The pace of change has moved from a gentle walk during the first Industrial Revolution, trotted through the second Industrial Revolution, moved to a canter with the impact of electronics and IT during the automation of the third revolution, and into a gallop with the digital revolution.

Hold onto your hats ladies and gentlemen; the ride is only getting faster.

When it comes to navigating the creation of a future-proof workplace, the skill of unlearning and relearning becomes even more paramount. The future-proof workplace requires that we:

- Fundamentally change our approach toward learning and talent development.

- Modernize our people, processes, and approach to talent management.

- Rethink our attitude to work, and, as a result, the design of workspaces.

We'll cover the third point in the following chapter, but for now we must future-proof your approach to learning, in your company and career.

THE HARE AND THE TORTOISE

The irony is that the industry of *learning* is perhaps the least prepared to meet the onslaught of the future-proof workplace. Traditional approaches to delivering early education have changed little in decades, if not hundreds of years.

Teachers are required to teach to a standard curriculum and topics to ensure that all students receive a similar baseline education. This approach creates a passive experience where students spend the day sitting in a classroom listening to their teacher tell them what they need to know. It cannot meet the needs of today's workforce, let alone the future-proof workplace.

If our current approach to education worked, we wouldn't have employers reportedly struggling to find employees with the right combination of skills, training, and credentials. Technology is a prime example of the skills shortage, with a near zero unemployment rate across all disciplines.

A global survey of 4,000 IT leaders by Harvey Nash, a global recruitment company headquartered in London, reported that 59 percent of employers said they face a skills shortage. The same percentage said that this skills shortage will prevent their organizations from keeping up with the pace of change.

Business leaders across industries are feeling the pain of this problem, too. Fifty-four percent of the nearly 700 respondents to a recent Harvard Business Review Analytic Services study said they lack the people and skills they need in order to compete effectively in the connected economy.[1]

A recent Deloitte survey reported 39 percent of company executives were either barely able or unable to find the talent their firms needed. Learning and re-learning is the twenty-first-century imperative.[2]

It's not just *what* we are learning that needs to change. We also need to transform the time it takes to acquire knowledge. In most western countries the standard school system looks something like this:

Primary and secondary education:	12 years
Graduate education:	4 years
Post-graduate education:	2 years
Total time:	18 years from start to finish

Contrast this with the oft-quoted Moore's Law, which states that computing power doubles every 18 months. The rate of change outside the academic world is lightning fast, the hare to the education tortoise. And we haven't even touched on the cost of acquiring that education.

Is it any wonder we have skills gaps in any role or industry, let alone in the STEM disciplines of science, technology, engineering, and math? It's not just because students aren't selecting these career paths; it's because when they do emerge from their studies, the environment they are joining has already moved on.

WELCOME TO THE NANO-DEGREE

Not only do we take too long to deliver a higher education but the twenty-first century has diluted the importance of a degree.

In 1950, approximately 3 percent of students went on to higher education. In 2016, this number was closer to 49 percent, breaking records in the United Kingdom for the number of applications received by universities. This pattern is repeated around the world with demand being fueled as more and more employers require an undergraduate degree for even the most entry-level roles.

The ripple effect continues with enrollment into post-graduate programs increasing as individuals seek to differentiate themselves from their peers. If our best and brightest are spending 12 years in secondary school, and then feel pressure to spend eight more years in higher education, our ability to respond quickly to change is vastly reduced.

"Come back in a decade, we'll have your engineers for you then" is not a viable business model when employers need them now.

Udacity is one of many new kids on the block when it comes to online learning and Massive Open Online Courses (MOOCs), much like Khan Academy and Lynda.com. What's transformational is that Udacity offers an alternative to the four-year degree: nanodegrees. It's advertising states, "Find free online courses, make a career change, or get a new job by completing a Nano-degree program."

A bold statement and one that is gaining traction. Given that the average job in Silicon Valley lasts 18 months you can see how a four-year degree might not match that need or demand.

Udacity's nanodegrees provide training and certification in technical subjects and skills (cybersecurity, software engineering, and web development, for example) and take 6 to 12 months to complete.

Before you dismiss the nanodegree as not having depth or credibility, consider that more than 4 million people in 168 countries have watched or completed Udacity programs.

We predict that the next iteration of graduate education will include not just timeline flexibility (traditional degree course condensed into a short time frame) but also content flexibility to allow learners to pick a more à la carte approach to the content of their degree.

CURIOSITY IN THE DRIVER'S SEAT

It's not just how we teach that has huge implications for the future of learning, it's also what we teach to meet the skills required of the twenty-first-century workforce.

Historically, learning has focused on the acquisition of knowledge, the *what* of content, and a deep specialization followed by the *how* of applying that knowledge in a given role. Usually the how is learned at the coalface (excuse the Industrial Revolution throwback) on the job—with new workers thrown in at the deep end of real-world experience.

However, spending four years learning the what of business seems archaic when we all have the ability to Google the answer to nearly any question. The future of learning needs to be tipped on its head, a focus on how knowledge is going to be used, the context in which learning will be applied, that will determine the priority of what needs to be learned.

We've all been asked at some point in our lives, "What do you want to be when you grow up?" or "Where do you see yourself in five years?" In both cases the expected answer is a job title—and a senior title at that. However, these questions don't reflect the rapid pace of change that has occurred in the design of the workplace.

New jobs are continuously emerging that didn't exist just a few short months or years ago: Uber driver, CrossFit instructor, Android or IOS developer, data scientist, 3-D printing engineer, or big data analyst to name just a few. For example, in just five years, from 2008 to 2013, more than 25,000 application developer jobs were created in the market,[3] and the number continues to grow. It's estimated that 65 percent of children entering primary education today will work in roles that don't currently exist.[4]

Now consider the job listings of the future, including robot repair technician and hologram stylist.

A single education, a linear education that is focused on developing the skills to succeed in a single expertise, is the legacy of a bygone era. While the process of learning is currently structured around the age of the learner, the reality is that most teenagers have access to almost any information at any time.

Scarcity drives value. Today, it's not information that's scarce, it's people who know how to use it at work.

As the organizational hierarchy changes and becomes flatter, the traditional vertical promotions that equated to career success become less relevant and less attainable. The future-proof differentiator is no longer seniority; instead it's a focus on horizontal and lateral moves—building a personal tool kit that allows us to add value wherever we work.

As industries come and go the need for new training becomes paramount. In the auto industry, thousands of workers are trapped in a shifting employment landscape by geography and lack of reskilling.

AT&T is facing the need to retrain tens of thousands of employees, and it is doing this in partnership with Udacity.[5]

Morag is the mother of three teenage boys and sees this change occur in real time. They don't want to wait to see what the teacher is going to share in their school classroom next week; they want to know now. They *can* know now.

Morag's on her fifth career, and an example of the importance of being a lifelong learner. If she dusts off her original career goals, after long-distance truck driver (honestly! she wanted to see the world) and space explorer (she's a huge *StarTrek* fan) she was planning to be an engineer. She actually enjoyed applied mathematics and physics.

Fate introduced her to a high school economics class and inspired the first change in direction. Instead of engineering she jumped into a finance career and nearly 15 years analyzing business plans, cashflow forecasts, and financial documents. From there, pivoted from the numbers side of the business into the people side, with a passion for leadership development.

More recently she's moved from solopreneur to entrepreneur, becoming an author and a speaker at industry and corporate events. Five careers in one lifetime and who knows what opportunities await!

A single degree in finance got her started, ongoing post-graduate studies in human resources management allowed Morag to pivot, and a commitment to lifelong learning is fueling current and future success. That original finance qualification is no longer relevant to the work she does. Not only is that degree old enough to drink, it's old enough to be a parent in its own right.

Learning agility and a healthy curiosity are going to be key skills for future success.

INTRODUCING THE "T" LEARNER

Now before you start burning your diplomas or college applications, we're not suggesting that formal learning should be thrown out with the proverbial bath water. There are fundamental skills that we all need to learn in order to have a basis from which to leap frog. The three Rs—reading, writing, and arithmetic—are a requirement. These are the entry-level minimum requirements that get us a seat at the table, our first project, our first job.

However, what will *keep* us at the table will be our ability to continue to learn and the breadth of learning that we embrace.

In the past, education could be described by "I"—deep knowledge and expertise in one area. Another ironic thought, the I of the traditional learner may explain the lack of collaboration and crossfunctional skills that many of our clients are trying to resolve. It's all about the I, the me-first focus instead of the horizontal we focus, but that's a thought for another time.

The shape of the future-proof learner is better represented by a truncated "T."

The increasingly complex workplace no longer fits neatly into one area of expertise. Instead, the need is there for all of us to become increasingly flexible, to have an understanding across disciplines.

Morag's first cars were a Citroën 2CV and an MGB Roadster (Google them if you don't recognize these). Those early years of car ownership regularly had her under the hood fixing the car, referring to the Haynes manual for pictures and step-by-step instructions. Even if Google existed back then, it would have been limited to a desktop PC and wouldn't have been much use in the garage.

Mechanical knowledge, an awareness of the impact of corrosion on the exhaust pipe, the cam belt, drive shaft, and a basic understanding of the internal combustion engine was enough to fix them as needed. And they did need fixing. Often.

Fast-forward to more than 30 years of car ownership and neither of us would even consider trying to work on our cars today. The complexity of the automobile industry has made it more difficult for the hobby enthusiast, unless we decide to relive our youth and buy a classic (a.k.a. simple) car. Today's car mechanic is a great example of the new T learner, with a deep knowledge of mechanics, in addition to engineering skills to support the electronics that have been added to the car's design.

The future-proof mechanic will need to extend that T wider as software expertise is required to support self-driving cars and the vehicles of tomorrow—deep expertise coupled with ever-increasing skills.

It's not just the car industry. The merging of technology in the health care industry has brought about transformative change. Surgeons leverage robotics to operate, and pharmaceutical companies are developing unique formulas to support personalized health care.

The T-shaped learner is the new world order, with transferable skills that are not specific to one job or one industry.

SOFT SKILLS FINALLY TAKE CENTER STAGE

While the nanodegree may provide a solution to a specific content need, the need for soft skills, also known as people skills, necessary for success will only increase.

In our work with clients around the world, the shortage of technical skills drives employers up the wall with frustration. But the far bigger cause for complaint is the lack of soft skills graduates seem to have.

Its social skills that underpin communication, collaboration, and teamwork—and these are rarely developed in a lecture. This is little surprise when students are scheduled from sunup to sundown and recess is seen as a luxury or used as a brief respite from the classroom.

Think about it in your own childhood. Recess is where we learned how to bond, build relationships, influence others, experienced conflict, and hopefully to resolve conflict.

A recent article on CBS MoneyWatch highlighted this lack of soft skills with employers complaining that new graduates may have the book smarts but are not work ready.[6] The same article stated that 60 percent of companies found new graduates lacked critical thinking skills and attention to detail, while 44 percent complained about the lack of writing proficiency, and 39 percent were critical of their public speaking ability.

Today there are laptops in every classroom, many schools no longer teach cursive writing (we called it joined-up writing in England—cursive sounds so very posh) and pupils type notes directly into their digital notepads. Ironically, research indicates that a step back to the old-fashioned pen and paper for note-taking may be needed. Some brain research shows that we are better able to recall items when we write them down rather than type them out.

Emotional intelligence and other core leadership skills are slowly being introduced to technical curricula. Learning opportunities that focus on team performance, not simply solo perform-ance, are being adopted. But the rate of change is slow and perhaps too slow.

It is anticipated that 40 percent of traditional jobs will be automated in the next 15 to 20 years to be replaced by . . . who knows what.[7] By 2020 it is anticipated that 36 percent of jobs across all industries will require complex problem-solving as a core skill, compared with the 4 percent that will need physical abilities.[8]

The World Economic Forum indicated that the top 10 skills needed for future success include intellectual reasoning, social and creative skills (such as intuition, critical thinking, influencing, and persuasion), abstract thought, and interestingly, the ability to apply ethical judgment. These are skills that can't currently be pro-grammed into computers or provided through artificial intelligence.

If you want to future-proof your own career, develop your interpersonal skills and stay one step ahead of the competition—and the robots!

COLLECTING CREDENTIALS INSTEAD OF CERTIFICATES

If the four-year degree is dead, then so is the certificate earned at the culmination of the program.

With the advent of MOOCs, anyone can access a higher education and any education online. Harvard Business School was one of the first to convert its classroom and on-campus programs to a virtual online MOOC. Stanford, MIT, and others are transferring their curriculum online, available to all, for free. Whether we're in Boston, the Outer Hebrides, or a small village in Africa, as long as we have access to the Internet we can access a Harvard program or any MOOC that captures our attention.

This learning is laudable—until you try to use MOOC learning to enter the workforce. At this time, employers are still stuck in the 1900s when it comes to their attitude about self-learning and online learning. Qualifications earned this way do not seem to be given same consideration or gravitas, and they are not as widely recognized. This attitude has to change because it's holding both employees and employers back.

The irony is that nanodegree certificates are considered lightweight and not necessarily proof that you *know* anything, whereas the traditional degree certificate may demonstrate book smarts but does little to show that you can actually *do* anything!

There has to be a major change in how we capture, assess, and value learning. If the four-year degree is not relevant, if the end of course certificate is no longer available, then a whole new educational industry will need to emerge. It's already in existence in some areas such as professional organizations that require continuing professional development, providing credits that are accumulated by attending various programs. This bite-sized learning is recognized by way of badges and credentials.

It was not so long ago that the press was mocking McDonald's for providing its staff members with stars on their name badges—stars that reflected their experience and learning. But we are all entering the era of the McCredential, a way to demonstrate our learning agility. The seeds of change are emerging, Arizona State University no longer differentiates in their transcripts between online or in-person studies. Starbucks offers all employees working 20-plus hours free online tuition after three months.

Are You Learning Agile?

Change is coming your way. What are you doing to stay ahead of the tsunami of change that's bearing down on you?

Hope is not a strategy that can be relied upon. If you believe that change will simply carry you along into the future, understand that this wave of change crushes anything in its wake.

Time to take an internship as a lifeguard or some online swimming lessons.

Modernizing Talent Management

If lifelong learning and midcareer relearning is the new normal, then the question becomes, *who owns the learning contract*?

Who provides the ongoing learning opportunities? How do we develop a future generation of leaders and managers who don't have the luxury of a 10-year apprenticeship but need to stay current for a 60-year working career?

Traditionally, the learning contract is owned by the employer and provided to a select few—the high-potential (HIPO) workers—or staff at certain leadership levels. While predictable career transitions will continue to exist, like moving from an individual contributor to a manager role, for most employees and employers a more flexible solution is needed.

A one-size-fits-all or a one-size-only-fits-a-few approach is no longer appropriate. The challenge is equipping the workforce with timely knowledge that allows individuals to respond to an ever-changing and increasingly complex environment. In the past, many managers learned through a period of apprenticeship (formal or informal), attending corporate learning events, and biding their time until they were promoted into their new role.

With the predictable surprise of the demographic time bomb—our baby boomers and Gen Xers retiring—we don't have much time before our millennials need to step up and take the reins.

The idea of having the top 20 is out. Everyone must be up to the task. Companies need to invest in every person to ensure that everyone can deliver on the innovation required—not just the top 20. Think about your strategy and stop thinking about your talent as *top*, *middle*, and *bottom*. Think which skills are required to achieve your strategy. *Who has them now, and who needs to develop expertise?*

Put plans in place like Rich Sheridan did at Menlo Innovations to pair people up to transfer needed skills and spark new ideas. Get rid of the old talent templates.

The challenge will be how do you provide 10 years of experience in 6 months—because talent today will likely not be with you in 10 years.

THE OLD DAYS OF TOO YOUNG

As a Gen-Xer, Morag, experienced the early stages of this conflict between readiness and old-world thinking; being told that she was too young to be a bank manager. The fact that she'd just graduated from the bank's accelerated management development program seemed to be lost on the powers-that-be, who happened to have created that very program.

In 20 years not much has changed. This same mind-set is being applied to our next generation of leaders and young managers—the assumption that age equates to success in the next role. We know this is not always true.

Not only is the time until moving to a new role shortening, but so is the patience level of millennials who are being asked to wait for advancement opportunities. If exciting work, project, or career opportunities aren't in regular supply in your company, millennials are more than ready to chase them elsewhere.

We need a different way to think about readiness for the big role or next promotion. How about right person, right role, right time? Now there's a novel idea.

WE CAN'T AFFORD A TRAINING BUDGET

Often training budgets are one of the first items to be cut when cash flow is tight. This may save a few dollars in the short-term but undermines the growth of the organization.

We've all heard the old cliché where the CFO turns to the CEO and says, "What if we invest in our people and they leave?" To which the CEO responds, "Yes, but what if we don't and they stay?"

In the future-proof workplace investing in your employees will be the differentiator that makes you an employer of choice.

Today there's a joint ownership for talent development.

If we are to remain ahead of the career curve, we need to invest in ourselves and push out of our comfort zones. We can't afford to leave this to chance or to our current employer.

Investing in ourselves, proactively learning, and seeking new experiences will differentiate us from other potential candidates.

LEARNING IS A CONTACT SPORT

Leadership and management development have come to a point of being too individually focused and elitist.

But there is a transition occurring from the old paradigm in which leadership resided in a single person, job title, or role. The future-proof mind-set is one where learning is a collective process that is spread throughout networks of people. It becomes a contact sport (metaphorically) as successful learners learn from each other.

The focus of talent management discussions will move from "Who are our leaders?" to "What conditions do we need for leadership to flourish in this team and this organization?" and "How do we spread leadership courage and capability throughout the organization?"

We need to cultivate a learning culture and a community of learners. Another reason why culture is so important to the twenty-first-century organization.

BUILD A LEARNING CULTURE

The best way to build a learning culture is to hire the right people.

We often hire for the boxes we can check: certain experiences or degrees instead of hiring for learning agility. How can this be incorporated into the hiring process?

Use behavioral interviewing, and look for clues in job candidates' previous experience. Do they demonstrate curiosity and learning agility? Or did learning stop when they received their diplomas? Some candidates might pass the test, but can they continue to learn?

Instead of looking at job-hopping as a red flag, look for the story behind the different roles.

Leaders need to build continuous learning into how we do business. In the twentieth century, continuing education was a checklist, not necessarily a learning exercise. Learning can happen every day in the office if we cultivate curiosity about what worked and what didn't. Instead of a blame game, we lower our defenses and learn from experiences.

Learning has to move from being an event to being a process. We need to build a culture of learning and an expectation of lifelong learning. Learning isn't just an HR function, it's a business priority. And a personal imperative.

We must avoid the quick and cheap approach to learning. Sure there are free online resources available, but a human connection with a real-life teachers is crucial.

In the future-proof workplace the role of the manager changes from sending an employee to a training course (or receiving surprised looks when the manager actually attends a seminar), to the role of mentor and coach.

A good coach provides access to the appropriate content and encourages application of the learning. The focus must shift from one of pure results to include a development mind-set. In doing so, employees and team members are more likely to receive effective feedback coupled with specialized training to help them increase their contributions to the team.

Everyone needs to be a coach and mentor. Coaching for the top echelons is an artifact of the twentieth-century. The twenty-first-century learning culture ensures that coaching is available for all.

Coaching circles are a powerful mechanism for peers to act as coaches and mentors to each other, and to help them learn and grow. Coaching has to become part of the culture and fabric of a learning organization.

If managers are to become mentors, how they are recognized and rewarded needs to include clear expectations that go beyond the financial metrics and include building talent and organizational capability. They also need to be held accountable for their own professional development.

If managers feel unprepared to become mentors, they must learn and step out of their comfort zones. Mentoring can be as simple as asking questions and really listening to the answers. Be genuinely curious about your team and about *What worked? What didn't?* and *Why?*

Curiosity may have killed the cat—but it can uncage the lion.

In team meetings ask, *What if?* and *What would it take?* Question the status quo and have the courage to admit you don't know the answer.

It's not just the manager's role to provide the coaching. Many organizations are introducing the concept of peer coaching and learning circles. Google is an example where more than 2,000 employees volunteered to teach a class or skill in one year alone.

Building a culture of peer learning and feedback accelerates the learning curve for everyone involved. But simply asking colleagues to coach each other will not deliver the change needed. An investment is required to build the capabilities of each and every employee to identify coaching opportunities, and to ask, listen, and respond.

In the same way, leadership development programs need to evolve to ensure they are providing the skills to support learning in a geographically diverse workforce.

A GLOBAL LEARNING MIND-SET

If the workforce is geographically dispersed, then so, too, are the leaders and managers. As a result, there are real challenges to bringing people together in real-time to attend a classroom-based program.

This doesn't mean that classroom training doesn't have a place. It does. Perhaps even a more vital place in the learning arsenal. If we want to learn human skills, reading a book or completing an online program will only get us so far. In years to come we'll be able to attend programs with our virtual headset. Until then don't underestimate the need to invest in bringing people together to allow them to collaborate, problem solve, make mistakes, succeed together, and build professional relationships.

With access to the Internet, problem solving becomes a different game—a series of critical thinking tests:

- Can I determine the core problem that I'm trying to solve?

- Do I know the appropriate question or keywords to enter into Google?

- Can I then assess the information returned to sort fact from fiction?

- And then, most critically of all, can I synthesize that information and apply it to solve the issue that I am facing right now?

Real-life challenges don't follow the formula in a textbook. Four years of book-learning and memorizing isn't enough. It's the in-the-moment learning through a process of search, analyze, and apply that matters. The traditional gap between academic learning and vocational learning needs to close.

The future-proof leadership development programs that we are developing in partnership with our clients span beyond the classroom. They include a breadth of learning resources including self-study, e-learning, virtual delivery (webinar or telephone conference), as well as real-world workshop-based learning. Our experience continues to show the importance of in-person opportunities to practice new skills in a safe environment.

If you want to learn how to develop your teamwork and collaboration skills, you can't do it alone. You have to practice communication with real, live, breathing humans.

Our future-proof programs are also designed to deliver lasting benefit during, and after, the learning experience— momentum that transfers learning from the theoretical into the real world. It's powerful. It's possible.

Simply wishing for a learning culture will not make it so. The future-proof workplace takes action to make it so.

CONTENT CURATION AND KNOWLEDGE MANAGEMENT

Institutional knowledge will be walking out the door during the next 10 years as baby boomers finally retire. The time to capture this knowledge is now, before it's too late.

Knowledge management matters, not because of the ticking demographic time bomb, but also because of the new flexible tour-of-duty mind-set of the millennials. People will be coming and going from your organization, and it would be naive to think you can retain someone forever. Instead, build the processes that help everyone to share knowledge while they are part of your team.

Whether it's organizational, academic, or vocational knowledge, learners need a personalized approach. Even if you have a library of 1,000 files, learners need help navigating this library. Companies need to curate the content and align it to the roles, certifications, and performance goals that the employee is being held accountable for.

Often the onboarding process for new hires or contract staff doesn't include access to key information. Many are simply thrown into the deep end and expected to figure it out. They will, but at what cost, in terms of mistakes, delays, or stepping on others' toes?

Shortening their ramp-up to productivity by providing access to knowledge *before* they join your team and in the critical first few weeks will differentiate your organization from others.

THROW OUT THE HR RULE BOOK

> Rules are for the obedience of fools and the guidance
> of the wise.
> —*Group Captain Sir Douglas Robert Steuart Bader CBE,*
> *DSO & Bar, DFC & Bar, FRAeS, DL, World War II*
> *fighter pilot, Royal Air Force*

Ask any HR professional what she thinks of the policies and procedures in her organization and most will acknowledge that many of them are dumb and difficult to enforce. These rules have unfortunately resulted in a reputation of human resources being a jobs-worth function trying to justify its existence.

There are many legal requirements designed to protect the employee from the unscrupulous employer, and, in some cases, protect the employer from an unscrupulous employee. We're not suggesting that these be ignored or thrown out; however, we would make a heartfelt plea for them to be simplified! The complexity of some of the legislation is time-consuming, for employee and employer alike, let alone the HR professional who acts as translator, mediator, and enforcer.

What we can't get our heads around is why so many of those rules and mind-sets regarding employees are still anchored in the end of the nineteenth century, designed for an illiterate workforce transitioning from the fields to the factories.

Rules appear as a result of the transgressions of a few and end up controlling the many. They certainly don't reflect an educated workforce or the needs of the future-proof workplace. Many rules actually limit learning, initiative, and creative thinking.

Do we really need a dress code that bans "spaghetti straps"? Women can wear skirts, but men can't wear shorts? Interesting. We assume kilts are okay?

Providing proof that a relative has died before you can attend a funeral and trying to place a finite time on grief (two days for a parent, one for a grandparent) is not only inappropriate, it's disrespectful. And do we really need a note from a doctor to prove we're sick? Let's clog up waiting rooms even more for minor ailments—while sharing the bugs.

Let's end policies that penalize people for being late but don't acknowledge the hours worked at the end of the day, in the evening, or during the weekend.

"Managing out" the bottom 10 percent of your workforce (remember this one?) only works if you can guarantee that the

10 percent you hire to replace them are better. And this flawed mind-set doesn't even take into to account the time required to learn the new role or the impact on others while they fill in for colleagues who were euphemistically let go.

And what's with spending hours debating nine-box positioning, when the only people who like a nine box are those in the top right-hand box? Everyone else is just annoyed with you (and their colleague) that they are not in the top right-hand box.

In a recent conversation with Josh Bersin, Principal and Founder of *Bersin by Deloitte*, he highlighted a recent study of managers and employees regarding performance reviews. Perhaps unsurprisingly, the study reports that 90 percent of the managers hated performance reviews and didn't see the business value. Employees had exactly the same opinion. He validated what we already knew; it's time to let the sun set on performance reviews as we know them, and the sun rise on a more effective conversation.

PERFORMANCE MANAGEMENT BECOMES THE PERFORMANCE MOMENT

In the twenty-first-century workplace performance management experiences a workplace makeover. Instead of a focus on goals and annual feedback mechanisms, teams and individuals are aligning around purpose, culture, and values. Gone is the annual review, a once-a-year conversation if you are lucky, in favor of real-time feedback that empowers and engages each person in the moment and treats them for what they are: adults.

Companies like Kelly Services, Dell, IBM, and even GE are doing away with the traditional twentieth-century approach. In a recent article, one Deloitte manager was quoted as saying,

"Performance reviews were an annual investment of 1.8 million hours across our business that didn't meet our needs anymore."

The individual focus of performance management and rewards is at odds with the team-based approach that is required going forward. In the fast-paced world of the twenty-first century, 12-month goals seem ludicrous, especially when manager and employee changes are happening regularly, let alone changing priorities and projects. Organizations are struggling to predict what their market and business will look like three to five years out, and annual cycles are becoming less defined. The planning horizons are coming closer, rolling 12-month cycles are the norm, and agile practices are needed.

It's time to think, and plan in dog years rather than calendar years. Short-term goals and milestones ensure meaningful feedback and progress in bursts while aligning to the overarching purpose and culture.

REWRITE THE TRAINING POLICIES

Most companies only provide training for a select few and exclude contractors or part-time workers. With a growing number of freelancers and contract employees this policy seems ridiculous. The implication is that part of your workforce gets to see the secret song sheet by which you operate, and everyone else has to hum along as best they can. Progressive organizations, like Deloitte, aren't just opening up their learning opportunities to their employees (whatever flavor they are), they're also opening programs to their customers and communities. Now there's a twenty-first-century idea!

Hours, months, and years are spent in the annual performance review cycle where managers are asked to grade their team and then told to lower their grades to meet an arbitrary curve or expectation from the C-suite. It feels more like junior high school than a workplace where responsible adults attend.

Thank goodness more enlightened companies are throwing out these preposterous time-sucking people processes and replacing them with adult-centric daily conversations. It's time we consigned some of our approaches to the history books where they belong.

Treat your employees for who they are—adults. Provide them with challenging goals and resources to achieve them. Then set them free to deliver the results. Where expectations are not being met, have the courage to provide the tough feedback, and give them an opportunity to step up. If they choose not to—or can't—you can decide to part ways. Either way it is a much more respectful and effective partnership.

WE ALL WANT TO LEARN

In our work with thousands of leaders across the globe, we can vouch for the fact that only a very small percentage of people are seeking to get by with the minimum of effort. Most employees want to do a good job, enjoy their work, build great relationships, and feel like they're connected to something bigger than themselves.

We dare you to take action.

If you can provide a future-proof workplace that engages curiosity, there will be no stopping you. We know where we'd choose to go to work!

FUTURE-PROOF YOUR COMPANY

- Take a hard look at your employee handbook—your people processes and policies. What can you throw out to unlock the shackles that are constraining your employees?

- How are you identifying learning agility in your current or future employees?

- How are you investing in your workforce and becoming an employer of choice?

- Are you a better version of yourself than you were yesterday? That's learning—for you and your team.

- Prepare for needing both legacy skills and future skills. Create a future-skills profile, and determine how the gaps will be filled. Will you build (develop) existing employees or buy (hire) new employees with those skills?

FUTURE-PROOF YOUR CAREER

- Seize the new opportunities when presented. What's the worst that happens when you try something new?

- Keep a learning journal. Reflect on what's working and what's not. What happened, and why do you think it happened that way? What's the *aha*, and what are you committed to doing as a result? If you write it down, you practice double-loop learning.

- Develop your mentoring skills by asking questions and not being quick to answer.

CHAPTER 9

Workspace

The Future-Proof Workspace

> You are a product of your environment. So choose
> the environment that will best develop you toward
> your objective.
>
> —W. Clement Stone

We *child-proof* our homes, but have we future-proofed our offices?

Office space is a major capital investment for most organizations, and an important one at that. The physical work environment affects just about every part of an organization: finances, culture, work process, productivity, employee satisfaction, recruitment, retention, and how employees interact with each other. It also impacts employees outside of work in terms of their commuting time to and from work.

Design your workspaces well and you'll have a twenty-first-century environment where people *want* to be, in which people can thrive. Design poorly and you have the office of the twentieth century, a destination employees *have* to go to.

The office of the past was designed for the sedentary desk-bound worker who arrived, sat at the same desk all day, and then left for home. The office of the future has to be designed around the active worker, encouraging people to get up and move around; whether it's standing at their desks or treadmill desks, a future-proof office supports relationship-cultivation and chance encounters with teams in other parts of the building.

The office needs to transform from a location *where* work is done to a destination and support for *how* it's done. From *where* we have to go, to somewhere we *want* to go. We must rethink our attitude toward work and the design of workspaces.

TIME TO TAKE BACK THE KEY TO THE EXECUTIVE WASHROOM

It wasn't so long ago that career success was measured by the size of your corner office, what floor you were on, or whether you owned a key to the executive washroom. These are status symbols of a bygone age, irrelevant to today's employee and remote workforce.

The new office is somewhere where it's easy to meet with colleagues, have fun, and yet also have a quiet space to get things done. It's an inviting environment that is adapted to accommodate everyone's needs, and where the magic of collaboration happens.

DOWN WITH THE CUBICLE FARM

If the goal is to drive collaboration and teamwork, then let's start pulling down the barriers that get in the way.

Cubicle farms have been a standard of the U.S. workplace for far too long. Unfortunately, in most cases, the egalitarian intent of everyone having a similar sized space and ready access to their colleagues has spectacularly backfired. Far too often you can walk the corridors but not see another person, unless they are doing the "meerkat bounce." You know the move, it's where maze-dwellers stand up in their cubicles, scan the horizon to see who is about, and sit right down again.

People use e-mail to chat with team members 20 feet away, and we wonder why there isn't real teamwork!

We recently visited a Silicon Valley campus. There were bikes everywhere and helmets to grab if you didn't have one. Workspaces included private pods where you could curl up and think and whiteboard walls where you could write ideas for others to build on. Great food trucks were at the sidewalk, along with dry cleaners, manicurists, and hair salons.

It was a village unto itself. Employees never had to leave, except perhaps to sleep. And we bet that will change, too.

This type of working environment is completely open: no walls, no hiding, and no excuses. Team members can simply raise their heads and talk to the person next to them. It leads to a much different environment where camaraderie and team relationships flourished.

Yes, private space is important. We personally hate hot-desking and not knowing where we'll be working. However, the cubicle farm has got to go and a new compromise reached. While an open plan environment may result in more spontaneous conversations, it can also drive others to despair with the noise and distractions. We still need quiet time away from the hubbub of the office and a private office to hold confidential conversations when needed.

Cubicle or office walls may not exist in the future-proof workplace. Instead they'll be replaced by the virtual wall of the noise-cancelling headset. We've had leaders tell us that they will often wear headphones that aren't actually connected to anything just to stop the interruptions and questions from colleagues when they are in an open plan environment.

The future-proof workplace has to balance the needs of the individual with the needs of the team. It must provide formal spaces as well as casual spaces where a different style of conversation will unfold, and increase the opportunities to learn from colleagues.

IT TAKES MORE THAN A PING-PONG TABLE

It's going to take more than bright colors, a foosball table, or the latest in standing desks for a team to embrace concepts of the future-proof workplace.

Silicon Valley firms have long been held up as the poster-child for the new-age office, offering a myriad of perks and environments for their employees. Whether it's gyms, professional kitchens with all-you-can-eat food, gaming facilities, music equipment and sound stages, bean bag chairs and slides, fancy coffee (with baristas), food trucks, or concierge services, no wonder people work long hours. Why would they want, or need, to be anywhere else?

It's a tough act to follow and has certainly helped to attract the talent those Silicon Valley firms need. However, there is hope for the small and medium-sized enterprise. It turns out that the bells and whistles may be just that: distractions from what is really creating the high-powered workplace of the twenty-first century.

As we work with our clients in these Silicon Valley firms, it is apparent how infrequently some of these perks actually get used. We repeatedly hear that while the ping-pong table is nice, the reality is that they rarely have time to use it during the work-day . . . because they are working!

Far more important to them is the sense of community and ability to make a difference through the work they do every day.

FROM WATER COOLERS TO WATERING HOLES

The result of pulling down the office walls and cubicles is an open space that needs to be deliberately designed as a space that encourages people to come, stop, and chat. In redesigning the office, many organizations are paying close attention to how employees move about the space, deliberately designing opportunities for chance encounters to occur where new ideas can be formed. Wearable technology allows employers to track employee movement in real time and, if used appropriately, adjust the office design accordingly. Big Brother really can be watching!

The common areas, traditionally centered around the proverbial water cooler (or tea kettle in the United Kingdom), have been redesigned as watering holes. These areas don't just provide beer on Fridays, but they are designed to be aesthetically appealing.

The watering hole encourages employees to linger, to make conversation and, more important, new connections, and, ultimately, to collaborate. In creating opportunities for unplanned interactions among employees both inside and outside the building, performance actually improves.[1]

One team of executives asked, "How can we change our space to get the sales staff running into colleagues from other departments?" In this case, the answer involved coffee. At the time, the company had roughly one coffee machine for every six employees, and the same people used the same machines every day.

The sales force commiserated with itself. Marketing people talked to marketing people. They stuck with their own tribes and unconsciously avoided going near strangers—their own colleagues!

The company invested several hundred thousand dollars to rip out the coffee stations and build fewer, bigger ones—just one for every 120 employees. It also created a large cafeteria for all employees in place of a much smaller one that few employees had used.

In the quarter after the coffee and cafeteria switch, sales rose by 20 percent, or $200 million, quickly justifying the capital investment in the redesign.

However, one of the most compelling transformations of the workspace is not just for those who use it in person, it's also designed to help remote employees feel connected to the mother ship. The future-proof workplace needs to invest in the full integration of technology, providing access to documentation, processes, systems, and people—24/7—and keeping us connected even when we work remotely.

ANYTIME, ANYWHERE

For the vast majority of workers, the office is not as important as it was in the past. The advent of technology has transformed every coffee shop, hotel foyer, park bench, or beach into a twenty-first-century office.

Remote workers need to be provided with all the necessary technology, training, and access to work anywhere, connecting seamlessly to office systems back at the traditional brick-and-mortar headquarters. This includes collaborative software like videoconferencing, instant messaging, and cloud-based file sharing, which allows people to avoid feelings of isolation and invisibility.

The twenty-first-century organization needs to provide these tools as well as clear permission to ignore them. The inability to switch off is at pandemic proportions; for many of us, our smartphone and e-mail is the last thing we look at before we sleep and the first thing we check when we awake.

Just because we can work anywhere and anytime doesn't mean we should. Our phones often receive more care and attention than our real-world relationships. You only have to look around a restaurant to see how many couples are more focused on their phones than each other. We support a move to reduce the number of after-hours e-mails and to ensure that vacation time is just that, an opportunity to focus on life.

Congratulations to the person who can design the app that blocks communication to and from the office at crucial times, much like the wireless microphones that don't (in theory) work when you step out of the conference hall to visit the restroom.

Wouldn't it be great if when we stepped out of work, whether the office or coffee shop, our phone knew that we were stepping into our lives—and didn't ring, flash, or vibrate to let us know of a new work message.

Since we seem unable to self-regulate we are starting to see legislation intervene. A law was recently passed in France that gives employees the "right to disconnect" from e-mail, smartphones, and other electronic devices once their working day has ended. French workers may now ignore business e-mails that arrive after hours with no recrimination, and no guilt. Now there's something we can all to aspire to!

No app is as effective as a clear company culture that values its peoples' free time.

FROM CORPORATE CAMPUS TO COMMUNITY CAMPUS

The notion that a single organization owns one space or a whole building for its own use is becoming a distinctly twentieth-century idea.[2] Zappos' executives used their headquarters to lead a local coworking experiment that launched in early 2012 and eventually grew to include nearly 200 stakeholders, among them Zappos employees, area residents, start-ups, independent workers, and others who shared the same physical premises. The spaces were improvised from a network of existing ones: a coffee shop, the courtyard of a Thai restaurant, an old church hall, the lobby of a casino, and an empty corporate apartment.

The proliferation of shared workspaces has continued unabated, with many small start-ups seeking out these collaborative zones. These organizations provide a membership-style service, with everything from a hot desk to a dedicated office available. Often, resources are provided not just in the city the business is located, but in any city where that corporate office suite is available.

Medium-sized organizations can now have an office footprint that many larger organizations might be envious of. In addition, these arrangements offer flexible usage, lower overhead costs, and the ability to tap into the expertise of other business owners who share the space.

Early results from Zappos showed that the small, shared nature of the space encouraged people to be more mobile, increasing chance encounters with other colleagues. After six months, data revealed a 42 percent increase in face-to-face encounters, a 78 percent increase in participant-generated proposals to solve specific problems, and an 84 percent increase in the number of new leaders. Ten new civic and local community projects were launched—including the Sunday Reset Project, a monthly event to promote healthful living.

DESIGNING FOR WELLNESS

The sharing economy epitomizes the open office—shared space, shared desks, shared everything, including germs when ill coworkers decide to come into the office. Designing the new workplace has to account for employee health and wellness, not just productivity.

Whether allowing pets in the office boosts or hinders productivity is an often-debated topic. As dog lovers, we can understand the desire to have Fido curled up at our feet. We're less convinced that bringing your cat to work would add anything other than the potential for a cat fight. Having pets in the office does reduce stress and can act as a social catalyst, a further opportunity for chance encounters or conversation starters.

Designing workspaces to facilitate employee wellness and encourage employees to walk around rather than sit for long periods of time is key for future-proofing your workplace. The twentieth-century office was more reminiscent of a battery farm for humans. We've all been told that sitting is the new smoking, with alarming health implications. Forward-thinking organizations are providing alternatives such as treadmill desks, standing desks, and a future that doesn't promote being chained to a desk all day. They are moving away from the back-to-back meeting schedule and requiring meetings to have a 10-minute transition time.

Providing opportunities for employees to reduce stress and be more aware of their health choices can only benefit them and, ultimately, the organization—a healthier bottom line for all!

SOCIAL AND ENVIRONMENTAL RESPONSIBILITY

The final piece in the workplace puzzle is the increased focus on social and environmental impact.

When it comes to community involvement, many organizations are throwing open their doors, encouraging employees to get out and connect with their communities. Salesforce.com[3] is consistently ranked as one of the top companies to work for. Employees have logged over 1.3 million volunteer hours since the company began this initiative. They receive seven paid days a year to volunteer, and all monetary donations are matched, dollar for dollar, by the company.

Twitter[4] doesn't just donate money to local nonprofits, employees regularly volunteer for a myriad of organizations. The company has donated laptops and other equipment to neighborhood centers and provided its office space for nonprofits to host events and fund-raisers. The company's latest endeavor is Twitter NeighborNest, a learning center that will be fully staffed by Twitter volunteers and will provide free computer classes (with child care) to anyone in the area.

Comcast Cares Day brings together more than 100,000 employees, families, friends, and local community partners who volunteer their time to make change happen. Comcast's intent is to make a difference globally and locally.

WHAT CAN YOU TRANSFORM TODAY?

It's unlikely that you can make an immediate move from your existing location or dramatically change the office layout overnight. However, there are steps you can take that will transform your office environment into one that more closely supports the needs of your future business and your employees.

Start by involving your employees and asking what kind of environment would support collaboration, innovation, and team building.

What would attract top talent and make those new employees want to come to work here? To what extent does your organization need public and private spaces? Open and closed? Flexible and fixed? Formal and Casual? Who else needs to have access to your office space? What do you want people to feel as they enter your office? What culture do you want to create? What behaviors do you need to harness or change?

The data will allow you to make informed choices about how you respond and redesign your workspace, whether you are on a budget or have a blank check. Ultimately, the future-proof workplace is one that allows all employees to be present (in person or virtually), to work together, learn together, and successfully deliver results.

If you don't have your future-proof workplace plan in place, you're already behind.

FUTURE-PROOF YOUR COMPANY

- Take a hard look at your workspace. Is it future-proof, or does it belong in a Museum? Based on your values, what changes can be made with no financial investment?

- Use the subject of workspace improvement as a way to open up dialogue on other issues as well.

- How does your workspace contribute positively to the culture you aspire to? How does it create obstacles to future viability?

- Host an office "painting party." What changes can you and your colleagues make with the resources and budget you have available?

FUTURE-PROOF YOUR CAREER

- What logistical changes can you make in your meetings to foster more productive communication? Experiment! Most people will appreciate the effort, and you'll learn valuable insights.

- Does your personal workspace create optimal productivity? What changes can you make to improve your workspace?

- Think about changing your workspace to allow you to connect and learn from others in new, enjoyable ways.

CHAPTER 10

Future-Proof Workplace

Waves of Change

> We must each lead our organizations, and
> ourselves, based on the reality of where we are
> today—not where we hoped to be. Leaders must
> have the courage to face reality and take action.
>
> —Linda Sharkey and Morag Barrett

They say the sense of smell is strongly connected to memory.

This probably explains why we can still remember our most recent cab ride, even though it was years ago.

The cab was called the day before to schedule an early pickup to the airport. The taxi pulled into the driveway right on time. As we squeezed into the backseat, several things stood out.

First, the plexiglass barrier between the driver and us seemed excessive and made it difficult to communicate. But we needed to catch a flight and had no other options. Prisoner transport would have to suffice.

The second thing we noticed about the culture of this rolling workplace was that there was plenty of legroom—for the driver, anyway. After all, he had to be in the car all day and needs to be comfortable.

185

Then there was the memorable smell of breakfast and lunch. And the aroma of an exhausted industry about to be passed by.

Reflecting on the current state of affairs of universal taxi experiences, Uber seemed to be worth a try for the next trip to the airport. The driver pulled up on time in a clean and fresh car with a bottle of water in the backseat. It felt like being driven by a chauffeur. A very different experience indeed. Needless to say, taxis are out and Uber is in.

Please don't misunderstand—we've met some wonderful cab drivers over the years and in many different countries. The point is that seemingly out of nowhere, the taxi industry has competition, and you and I have options. This is another example of an institution failing its people.

Uber feels different, in our experience, anyway. It disrupted the market like it was standing still. Because the market *was* standing still.

Have you even stood in knee-deep water at the beach, breathing the salty air, only to be knocked over by that wave you didn't see? That must be how the cab companies felt.

And the response from the taxi industry has been fascinating. In general, its first reaction was denial, followed by demands for more government regulation to quell what it viewed as unfair competition. A typical twentieth-century reaction to change.

Instead of taking a hard look at how customers viewed its service and brand—and making adjustments—it fought to keep the status quo. The modern day equivalent of throwing a clog in the loom. The taxi industry chose to look for ways to force people to use taxis and attempted to get rid of Uber and other such disrupters through legislation and strikes. And frankly, the industry was slow to take action until it was too late. The disruption was the new normal.

THE HUMAN WAVE

Others often look at disruptive companies like Uber as tech companies, whereas we like to look at them as human companies—focused on using technology to create win-win relationships and solutions for customers. They aren't simply focused on the digital interface and connecting systems, processes, and customers in a new way. They are also focused on the human interface, the customer experience.

Customers are people, by the way. Everyone in business needs to be reminded of that regularly—us, the authors, included.

Employees and colleagues are people. So, too, are vendors and cab drivers. Change often feels threatening, and when our livelihoods are threatened, we can often react with a fight or flight response. Helping people to navigate the waves of change is our role as leaders in the twenty-first century.

This practice requires intentional effort and in some cases a real shift in mind-set. We must pay attention to the human element of change and not have our heads down in the sand—or in our devices.

The waves of change are always driven by human desire. These waves will keep breaking on the world of work, with increasing speed and force. The factors we've brought to light are not just tides that come in and go out, leaving everything as it was. These six factors are transforming the landscape, and they will transform your workplace.

As leaders, your company and career can be wiped out by change. Or you can ride the wave.

But there's a third alternative. You can be the wave.

LEADING THE FUTURE

Do something. Make waves. That's what leaders do.

Great leaders don't just agitate for the sake of making their presence known. They make positive waves of change that ripple throughout an organization.

We suggest the first step is to take a hard look at your leadership results—both in leading yourself and leading others. Are you a leader who believes you have all the answers because you have so much experience? Do you believe that you have to tell people what to do or they won't get it right?

If this is what you discover, you're in the leadership riptide, and you must break free if you are to survive.

Fast data and almost-instantaneous market feedback mean that leaders will be under more scrutiny than ever. What does honest scrutiny of your company and yourself reveal? Where does change need to occur? Where are you stuck in the twentieth century?

Leaders must have a clear set of guiding values and purpose for the twenty-first century.

We want to remind you again about our friend Walter McFarland and what he said about great leaders. He shared that they have three things in common. "The first big theme was passion," he told us recently. "When you read the statements of the people who accomplished the most, it didn't happen by chance. They didn't achieve because they were obsessive or compulsive. They did it because they cared about it, right down to their very DNA."

The second thing he shared was that great leaders "seemed consistently able to attach whatever their task was to that higher purpose. It was about changing something in a bigger and better way. It was about the opportunity for people to engage and make a real difference in the makeup of their organizations."

And the third piece was that "somehow, in the midst of doing these global, galactic big things, they found time to develop people. They did that without exception."

We believe the future will be built by leaders who build up others and have a heart to serve others. It might be time for you to ALTRR your leadership behavior after you have made serious examination. What does ALTRR stand for?

Ask for ideas, input, and suggestions. Dig deep to gain understanding of different views.

Listen and learn from the responses.

Think about what you have heard, and formulate some conclusions regarding your purpose.

Respond to others with what you believe is right, and engage them in the response.

Repeat this approach as a way of tapping into the power of perspective, and make it a habit—a cultural cornerstone.

ALTRR will open your eyes to better ways of doing things before you react with a twentieth-century response.

CULTURE DETERMINES INNOVATION AND SPEED

Culture is not what you *hope* employees, clients, and communities think about your company—it's what they actually think.

Having an outside-in, customer view is essential. This perspective makes your company the wave—and keeps you from being knocked over by another wave. This is what keeps a culture fresh, flexible, and innovative.

Change is required, yet change exposes cultural problems that nobody talked about before. That's why mergers are often so tumultuous—all the unspoken rules suddenly collide.

If you want to grow, you have to understand what your culture really is, not what you wish it to be. Some leaders won't do that. Those leaders won't survive. And whether or not you have "leader" in your job description, you're a leader.

You know there's an intangible factor that needs to be made tangible: culture. The difference between success and failure is people who are willing to wrestle with culture. Will you be one of those people?

In reading this book you know that corporate culture impacts just about every aspect of your organization. It dictates how you behave, decide direction, teach and learn, organize your office space, and leverage technology. Culture can either constrain or unleash you.

It's time for the elephant in the room to be escorted out by security.

It's not about the slogans and values statements but how those values statements are put into action in everyday decisions and everyday behaviors.

We believe the future will be built in company cultures we love.

NAVIGATING WITH PURPOSE

Your company needs clear purpose. Purpose is the wind in your company's sails. And arriving on that clear purpose requires a view toward the future. Is your purpose noble and helping mankind? Or are you still in mourning for the "good old days" and trying to hang onto the past? Are you and your company primarily driven by financial goals?

In this case we'll break our no-crystal-ball rule and say it's easy to predict which kind of companies will be thriving in a decade.

A workplace needs a human purpose, derived from human needs and values. Beyond profitability, what drives your organization and you, personally? Is your organization's purpose future-proof?

Tap into that deep current and let purpose guide future decisions and initiatives. When you define your purpose, as a company or an individual, you create a barometer to judge your decisions.

The twentieth century engaged the mind—the logic of supply and demand, being first to market, the bottom line. Success in the twenty-first century goes deeper, it goes broader, to engage not just our minds but our hearts.

A purpose with passion inspires everyone to go the extra mile to deliver an exceptional experience for their customers, internal and external. It makes every employee, whether they are cleaning the bathrooms or setting policy, understand the greater good they are creating.

We believe the future will be built by purposeful individuals.

OUR RELATIONAL FUTURE

Business is personal.

How many billions of dollars in business transactions are secured, or lost, because of the quality (or lack thereof) of personal relationships? On a geopolitical scale, we can measure the effect in trillions of dollars and sadly, in life-and-death struggles.

Damaged relationships damage bottom lines.

Sure, we can yell at Siri or kick an ATM and they will continue to dutifully follow their programming, however flawed. Assembly line workers can curse the robots, but those machines will keep on welding. But just as customers are human, so are you and your colleagues.

Relationships matter. We sometimes forget that in the busyness of business.

If your core belief is that "business is business," you will probably have an unconscious belief that there are a different set of rules for colleagues than for personal relationships. Those lines are not only blurred, they disappeared decades ago.

You cannot be successful in business, or in life, unless you are successful in cultivating winning relationships. This has always been true and is especially true in the twenty-first century.

We believe the future will be built on Ally relationships.

FUTURE INCLUSION

Diversity is not the goal. Diversity can be measured and achieved through percentages.

Inclusion is an attitude, a worldview, not a number. And we all fall short to some degree.

If you agree, the place to start future-proofing your company is to avoid the temptation to pat yourself on the back because of numbers, and open your heart to look for hidden bias.

This entire book could be viewed as several possible initiatives, or checklists, for your company. But in reality, every chapter is geared to this goal: putting heart back into your work.

Anything that hinders healthy collaboration hurts us all. What solutions have eluded humanity because we haven't connected on a more human level? What possibilities become real when we break down barriers and unify with a common purpose?

We believe the future is inclusive.

RESISTANCE IS FUTILE—TECHNOLOGY

Let's be clear about our vision for the future of work. It is not a scene from *The Matrix*, with humans tethered to machines, all working for the good of some unknown entities.

Ironically, the digital revolution is placing the human side of business at the forefront. The more technology we possess, the more our need for human connection becomes apparent. And, the more we can choose to use technology to enhance communication, the better our working relationships will be.

Every business is now a digital business. Yet the future of work can, and must, have a heart.

Technology is the primary impetus for a major shift to shape how work gets done and careers evolve. Shiny objects are engaging, but shiny objects that take communication and human connection to another level are game-changing.

In our experience, successful leaders are those who balance not just the *what* of technology but also the *how*, the *who*, and the *where*.

We believe the future will use technology to enhance our humanness.

CURIOUS LEARNERS

Education desperately needs to be future-proofed.

If a job requires a four-year degree, by the time a candidate completes the coursework that job and the entire workplace landscape will have changed dramatically.

What if we had the courage to question educational norms (yes—all of them), and leveraged technology to make learning practical?

On a personal level, we must also embrace the fact that each of us has a personal responsibility to nurture our curiosity and to be lifelong learners. What are you doing to learn valuable skills that will future-proof your career?

As managers, leaders, and HR professionals, we must face the inherent bias we have toward some institutional educational models and be willing to embrace pragmatic solutions to empower our workforce and future-proof our companies.

We believe the future needs new ways of teaching curious learners.

THE FUTURE-PROOF WORKSPACE

Instead of thinking a vibrant company culture can be built with a new color of paint and fancy desk chairs, understand that a workspace is the reflection of culture.

In other words, foosball and fireman poles are only a temporary distraction, unless the changes reflect an authentic expression of purpose and values and are evidenced by how we treat each other.

We believe the future workplace will be a community not a cubicle farm—a place where people truly engage, interact, and respect each other for a greater common good.

WORK MATTERS

We spend a large portion of our existence at work, thinking about work, stressing about work.

While the average workweek is supposed to be 40 hours, for most of us the reality is 60 hours or more. We plan our lives around work, and for many of us work is the focal point around which everything else revolves—including personal relationships. Work can be a creative outlet and a healthy challenge.

Work is clearly a big deal. And yet work gets a bad rap. We complain about the Monday morning blues, hump day Wednesday, thirsty Thursday, thank goodness it's Friday (a.k.a. POETS day: Pop Off Early, Tomorrow's Saturday). Not sure what we should be griping about on Tuesday.

And yet we all still need to work. Left to our own devices we like to produce, create, and contribute. But the nature of work is changing. Work will become more egalitarian, with everyone valued for what they contribute to the common good and not how high they are in the corporate hierarchy.

Much of what we experience today and know as "work" is rooted in the methods and philosophy of the Industrial Revolution. But we are no longer in the mechanical age; we are in the midst of the digital and human age.

It's time to retire the whole work/life balance debate. It was a ridiculous concept in the best of times; today, the premise of *all work with a little dash of life* no longer sits comfortably.

Instead, let's all embrace life, with intermittent bursts of work and productivity!

They are forever interconnected. One does not happen without the other, but if we embrace flexible working and family-friendly policies, why not go all the way and actually embrace *employee-friendly* policies? If we will, work can become someplace where we want to be, not where we have to be—a place that helps us to thrive, contribute to the organization's purpose, and leave a legacy that benefits all.

What does this mean for the future of work?

What are the new skills that will be needed?

What skills may become obsolete?

Are you going to have a robot manager?

Will you supervise a robot team?

When and where does your work need to occur?

How will you braid your work and life so that it is seamless and adds the value you need?

Work matters, but the question is, *does your work matter?*

Business matters, but *will your business matter next year?*

TIDAL WAVES

Raise is tapping into an estimated 80 billion dollar market allowing shoppers to buy or sell unwanted gift cards—without owning any retail space.

Airbnb has more rooms available than the largest hotel groups in the world. All with a core staff of fewer than 1,000 employees and without owning any real estate.

Beepi is transforming the used car market, inspecting the car—at your home—and then introducing buyers and sellers without the need for a garage forecourt or a visit to the local car dealership.

Uber has more than three times the annual revenue of the entire taxi and limousine industry—all without owning any vehicles.

Upwork has more than 12 million registered freelancers, delivering more than 1 billion dollars of work annually for more than 5 million clients around the world.

Blue Apron and Freshly are transforming home cooking by delivering meal kits and recipes to your door. Much more convenient than worrying over the answer to "what's for dinner?" and having to dash around the grocery store.

Khan Academy and Udacity are transforming the education industry. Khan Academy provides free learning, for everyone, anywhere. Udacity is at the heart of the nanodegree movement with its corporate purpose being "to bring accessible, affordable, engaging, and highly effective higher education to the world. We believe that higher education is a basic human right, and we seek to empower our students to advance their education and careers." Education is a lifelong experience.

As the saying goes, "we ain't seen nothing yet."

We're in for more massive changes in work, business, and our careers.

OVERWHELMED?

Future-proofing your company and career might be challenging at times, but it's possible.

You'll need to take a radical look in the mirror in order to see eye to eye with your colleagues, but it's worth it.

Besides, what's the alternative?

If you'll take time to review your notes at the end of each chapter, or make those notes if you skipped over them, you can begin making small steps for positive change. Don't put this book away or give it away to a colleague until you tackle these important action steps! You can also find printable PDFs and other resources at www.futureproofworkplace.com.

THE FUTURE

Are you envisioning the future?

Are you talking about it?

Do you see both the scary scenarios and the possibilities to change work, and change lives, for the better?

Are you taking action to embrace the future?

> Until you make the unconscious conscious, it will control your life and you will call it fate.
> —*Carl Jung*

FOLLOW OUR THREE Es

Explore: what does the future of work look like for you and your company? Define your purpose (personal and professional) and involve others in embracing the future of work.

Experiment: Create rapid learning environments, use data and analytics to inform your approach.

Execute: Dump the policies and procedures rooted in the twentieth century and test the new ways of working.

But most important, *act*! Identify the one thing you can do today to prepare for tomorrow. You're not just leading a digital revolution. You're also leading a people revolution!

The biggest challenge is to recognize that the future of work is not tomorrow. The future of work is today. The longer you hesitate, the bigger the gap you will need to overcome.

And the sooner you begin the further ahead you'll be.

Notes

Chapter 1 Surviving and Thriving in Turbulence

1. Mark J. Perry, "Fortune 500 Firms in 1955 v. 2015; Only 12% Remain, Thanks to the Creative Destruction That Fuels Economic Prosperity," AEIdeas, October 12, 2015, https://www.aei.org/publication/fortune-500-firms-in-1955-vs-2015-only-12-remain-thanks-to-the-creative-destruction-that-fuels-economic-growth.

2. Emma Seppälä and Kim Cameron, "Proof That Positive Work Cultures Are More Productive," *Harvard Business Review*, December 1, 2015, https://hbr.org/2015/12/proof-that-positive-work-cultures-are-more-productive.

3. Charles Duhigg, "What Google Learned from Its Quest to Build the Perfect Team," *New York Times*, February 25, 2016, http://www.nytimes.com/2016/02/28/magazine/what-google-learned-from-its-quest-to-build-the-perfect-team.html?_r=0.

Chapter 2 Leadership

1. Phil Dourado, "The Speech that Changed the Course of the Civil War," The Leadership Hub, April 2, 2012, www.theleadershiphub.com/vault/blogs/speech-changed-course-us-civil-war.

Chapter 4 Purpose

1. "Avon Values and Principles," www.avoncompany.com/aboutavon/history/values.html#mission.

2. Graham Kenny, *Harvard Business Review*, September 3, 2014.

Chapter 5   Relationships

1. Anat Lechner, "The Science of Relationships," *Time* Special Edition, 2016, p. 91.
2. Google definition of "work," www.google.com/webhp?sourceid= chrome-instant&ion=1&espv=2&ie=UTF-8#q=definition+of+work.
3. "Employee Engagement and Retention Report," 2013 Kelly Outsourcing and Consulting Group, www.kellyocg.com/uploadedFiles/ Content/Knowledge/Kelly_Global_Workforce_Index_Content/ Employee_Engagement_and_Retention_2013_KGWI.pdf.
4. Lauren Weber, "One in Three U.S. Workers Is a Freelancer," *Wall Street Journal*, September 4, 2014, http://blogs.wsj.com/atwork/ 2014/09/04/one-in-three-u-s-workers-is-a-freelancer.
5. "Garden City Movement," Wikipedia, https://en.wikipedia.org/ wiki/Garden_city_movement; "List of Quaker Businesses, Organizations and Charities," Wikipedia, https://en.wikipedia.org/wiki/ List_of_Quaker_businesses,_organizations_and_charities.
6. "Non-Financial Reporting," European Commission, January 7, 2016, http://ec.europa.eu/finance/company-reporting/non-financial_ reporting/index_en.htm#news.
7. Lynda Gratton, "Linda Gratton Investigates: The Future of Work," *Business Strategy Review*, Q3, 2010, www.lyndagratton.com/uploads/ BSR%20-%20LG%20investigates%20the%20FOW.pdf.
8. Jason Dorrier, "There Are 7 Billion Mobile Devices on Earth, Almost One for Each Person," Singularity Hub, Singularity University, February 18, 2014, http://singularityhub.com/2014/02/18/ there-are-7-billion-mobile-devices-on-earth-almost-one-for-each- person.

Chapter 6   Inclusion

1. "List of Women CEOs of Fortune 500 companies," Wikipedia, https://en.wikipedia.org/wiki/List_of_women_CEOs_of_Fortune_ 500_companies.
2. "Susan Boyle," Wikipedia, https://en.wikipedia.org/wiki/Susan_Boyle.

Chapter 7 Technology

1. "Hot-Fire Tests Show 3-D Printed Rocket Parts Rival Traditionally Manufactured Parts," National Aeronautics and Space Administration, Washington DC, July 24, 2013, www.nasa.gov/exploration/systems/sls/3dprinting.html.
2. Stefan Lindegaard, "Critical Lessons, Facts on Open Innovation," 15inno, June 2, 2010, www.15inno.com/2010/06/02/criticalfacts lessons.
3. "Common External Power Supply," Wikipedia, https://en.wikipedia.org/wiki/Common_external_power_supply.
4. "Few Have Witnessed What You're About to See," Galaxy Zoo, https://www.galaxyzoo.org (accessed July 16, 2016).
5. "About Flash Teams," Stanford University, 2014, http://stanfordhci.github.io/flash-teams/about.html.

Chapter 8 Learning

1. "I.T. Talent Crisis: Proven Advice from CIOs and HR Leaders," *Harvard Business Review*, June 13, 2016, https://hbr.org/sponsored/2016/06/i-t-talent-crisis-proven-advice-from-cios-and-hr-leaders.
2. "Demand Grows Abroad for Finance to Serve as Business Partners," *Wall Street Journal*, July 25, 2013, http://deloitte.wsj.com/cfo/2013/07/25/demand-for-finance-to-serve-as-business-partners-grows-abroad.
3. "Agiletown: The Relentless March of Technology and London's Response," London Futures, Deloitte and the University of Oxford, November 2014, p. 10, https://www2.deloitte.com/content/dam/Deloitte/uk/Documents/uk-futures/london-futures-agiletown.pdf.
4. Niall Dunne, "How Technology Will Change the Future of Work," World Economic Forum, https://www.weforum.org/agenda/2016/02/the-future-of-work.
5. Quentin Hardy, "Gearing Up for the Cloud, AT&T Tells Its Workers: Adapt, or Else," *New York Times*, February 13, 2016,

www.nytimes.com/2016/02/14/technology/gearing-up-for-the-cloud-att-tells-its-workers-adapt-or-else.html?_r=0.

6. Jonathan Berr, "Employers: New College Grads Aren't Ready for Workplace," *MoneyWatch*, May 17, 2016, www.cbsnews.com/news/employers-new-college-grads-arent-ready-for-workplace.
7. *The New Work Order* (Melbourne, Australia: Foundation for Young Australians, 2015).
8. "The Future of Jobs," World Economic Forum, 2016, https://www.weforum.org/agenda/2016/01/the-10-skills-you-need-to-thrive-in-the-fourth-industrial-revolution/ or http://www3.weforum.org/docs/WEF_FOJ_Executive_Summary_Jobs.pdf.

Chapter 9   Workspace

1. Ben Waber, Jennifer Magnolfi, and Greg Lindsay, "Workspaces That Move People," *Harvard Business Review*, October 2014, https://hbr.org/2014/10/workspaces-that-move-people.
2. Ibid.
3. "100 Best Companies to Work For," *Fortune*, 2016, http://fortune.com/best-companies/salesforce-23.
4. Michal Lev-Ram, "Welcome to the Twitterloin, Where Tech-Savvy Cool Meets Gritty Hood," *Fortune*, March 5, 2015, http://fortune.com/2015/03/05/twitter-office.

ACKNOWLEDGMENTS

It is a privilege to have worked with so many great leaders and companies throughout our careers, and we want to thank all of them for their insights and lessons that contributed to the richness of this book. We also want to thank all the people that had faith in us that we could create this book that would add so much to the future of work.

Particular thanks to all the people who were guests on Linda's radio show, iLead the Leadership Connection with VoiceAmerica. Everyone on the show shared such incredible insights into the changing nature of work. Each person helped us shape our thinking on how to future-proof yourself and your workplace now.

There are just too many to list. You can listen to all of the shows and find additional resources by going to our website www .FutureProofWorkplace.com. We are so grateful for their contributions to our thinking and willingness to share. It was an outstanding experience to interview all the guests and thought leaders who gave of their time.

Robert Ciolino of VoiceAmerica deserves a big shout-out for encouraging Linda to add radio host to her resume and for helping us think about formulating this book. Robert was a great coach and mentor. He is simply a fountain of ideas!

And finally, Marshall Goldsmith is recognized as a top leadership thinker by the Thinkers50 and is a world-famous coach. He has supported Linda throughout her career and helped Morag on her last book. We are so grateful for your guidance and great willingness to give back and give forward. You have been a total mentor and inspiration in this chapter of our careers.

We are privileged to have had the experiences and opportunities to get to work with so many outstanding people who have made a difference in the world of work. All of you are truly leaders of the future. You are the people who are bringing the human heart back into the workplace, and you all know who you are.

We would also like to especially thank Mike Loomis, who encouraged us and provided us thought leadership throughout this effort. Mike is truly a great sounding board and helped us shape our thinking and ideas in an incredible way. Without Mike we don't think we would be here today sharing this book and the stories that make it live.

It is a difficult task to shape a book like this, especially when working with a coauthor. However, we know we couldn't have done it without each other. We were supports to each other. We acted as muses and mentors to each other and made a difficult task intellectually stimulating and fun. Needless to say, Mike Loomis was a big part of that experience and "mind meld" as well.

We are excited that this book is no longer in the future, but here, today. We are much enriched because of writing it and have built some formidable relationships and connections that will live on.

WELCOME TO THE FUTURE OF WORK

L inda and Morag are actively working with companies, teams, and individuals committed to understanding and taking action to future-proof their careers and organizations.

Linda and Morag are regularly invited to speak at events around the world. Their fast-paced, informative, and interactive keynotes and workshops will add impact to your next corporate or association event.

Drawing on their experience working with leaders across the globe, they will inspire your participants and promote discussion and new thinking. As a result, your leaders will gain pragmatic how-to tools and resources that they can put into immediate use.

For information on speaking engagements, workshops, and thought-leadership, please visit: www.FutureProofWorkplace .com or e-mail us linda@futureproofworkplace.com or morag@ futureproofworkplace.com

ABOUT THE AUTHORS

LINDA SHARKEY, PHD

Linda Sharkey is a trusted transformational expert, author, speaker, and global leadership development coach.

Through her programs and no-nonsense approach, she helps create high-potential leaders and shapes company culture. Linda has deep experience working with Fortune 50 companies, and held senior human resource executive positions at Hewlett-Packard and GE Capital.

Her coauthored book *Winning with Transglobal Leadership* was named one of the top 30 best business books for 2013.

Dr. Sharkey is an inspiring keynote speaker at many global events, including the Global HR Academy with the Conference Board and the World Human Resources Development Conference, where she was honored with the Super Women Achievement Award.

LindaSharkey.com

MORAG BARRETT

Morag Barrett is the author of the best-selling book *Cultivate—The Power of Winning Relationships*. She is also the founder and CEO of SkyeTeam, an international HR and leadership development company.

As a sought-out speaker and leadership development expert Morag brings a pragmatic perspective to her work with forward-thinking organizations, from start-up to FTSE 100 and Fortune 100 companies. She is a regular contributor to Entrepreneur.com, CIO.com, and the American Management Association.

Prior to founding SkyeTeam, Morag held leadership positions at Level 3 Communications and NatWest Bank where she advised international organizations on their corporate strategy and growth plans. Originally from the United Kingdom, she has experience working with more than 3,000 leaders in 20 countries on 4 continents.

SkyeTeam.com

ALSO BY THE AUTHORS

LINDA SHARKEY, PHD

Operating and expanding business units offshore, selling in foreign markets, and managing global supply chains are just three of the many challenges that emphasize the importance of leaders that can transcend borders.

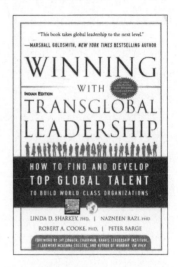

Winning with Transglobal Leadership will help prepare your organization to meet this need head-on with a framework for developing and training leaders that best fit your global growth strategies.

The book combines insights from a global team of author-experts. Together, they draw on an impressive range of resources—extensive original research, interviews with world-class high-performing executives, and decades of combined experience as senior executives, researchers, and consultants—to deliver an easily implemented process for assessing your organization's global capability and developing the leaders who will drive success. Inside *Winning with Transglobal Leadership*, you will find:

- Guidance on measuring and evaluating your organization's capacity to compete globally

- Five behavioral dimensions that global leaders need to develop

- Keys to assessing leadership candidates early in their careers

- The "Transglobal Leadership Matrix," a tool for taking stock of your own skills and behaviors

At a recent World Economic Forum in Davos, Switzerland, numerous CEOs in attendance cited a growing need for talent that could function successfully in new and emerging global markets. For leaders and managers, HR and training specialists, or anybody doing business today, *Winning with Transglobal Leadership* is the definitive handbook on satisfying the demand for specialized leadership skills—now and in the years to come.

HOW TO COMPETE AND WIN IN TODAY'S BUSINESS ENVIRONMENT

Real-life business experience, actionable advice, and fact-based evidence—that's what sets *Optimizing Talent* apart from every other book on talent management.

Summarizing research conducted within more than four hundred Fortune 1000 companies, the authors:

- Provide an integrated Talent Optimization Framework™ and Survey for diagnosing talent optimization gaps.

- Demonstrate which actions drive integration and optimize talent.

- Show the improved results achieved by organizations that excel at each level in the Framework.

Topics include the importance of engaged leaders and a supportive culture, a detailed operating system that creates the foundation for high-performance talent, and the ability to measure meaningful results. In addition, each chapter includes case studies and a checklist so readers can easily implement similar programs and ideas at their own organization.

Optimizing Talent is a practical call-to-action for all levels of business leaders, managers, talent practitioners, and scholars and will help you think strategically about creating a talent-rich organization.

The *Optimizing Talent Workbook* will guide you through a hands-on, practical application of what you learned from *Optimizing Talent: What Every Leader Needs to Know to Sustain the Ultimate Workforce*. Not only will you learn to apply the Optimizing Talent Framework in your organization, you'll find that we've expanded on the foundation of Optimizing Talent to include the incredibly valuable topics of talent branding and neuroscience, as well as case studies of companies that have used the framework to great success. The *Optimizing Talent Workbook* provides a step-by-step strategic implementation approach for developing and retaining the best talent whatever your business!

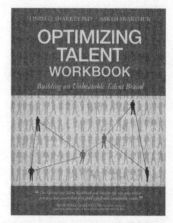

MORAG BARRETT

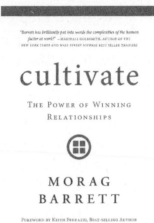

- Have you been blindsided by a colleague's words or actions?

- Are you plagued with the worst of office politics, shifting alliances, and silos?

- Are your results impacted by poor communication or mis-aligned expectations?

- Do you need to establish rules of engagement that enhance relationships and accelerate success?

In *Cultivate*, SkyeTeam CEO and author Morag Barrett provides a simple but effective model for diagnosing the health of your relationships at work and recommends steps to develop your ability to form Ally Relationships.

Use *Cultivate* to:

- Identify your critical relationships and stakeholders.

- Apply the Relationship Ecosystem™ to diagnose the health of your relationships.

- Examine how context, culture, and communication impact your relationships.

- Understand how and why an Ally mind-set is vital to your career success.

- Apply relationship strategies to strengthen your professional relationships.

Whether you're a seasoned leader or starting out in the workplace, you'll see the world of work in a whole new way. Morag delivers practical lessons and tools to navigate every relationship in your career.

INDEX

change (*continued*)
  technology for, 8–9, 16, 120, 121–122, 193–194
  in workplace culture, 8–9, 11–12
  workplace factors of, overview, 8–17
Civil War, desertion during, 29–31
collaboration. *See* relationships; teamwork
collaborative software, 135–136, 176–177
colleagues, relationships with, 78, 90–92
Comcast Cares Day, 180
"command and control" leadership, 10, 22–23
common areas, in workspaces, 175–176
communication. *See* relationships
communities
  community campuses as workspace, 178–179
  learning in, 158
  relationships with, 78, 93–94
  sense of community in workspaces, 174–176
Connect+Develop (Procter & Gamble), 130
consistency, of leaders, 37–38
content curation, for learning, 162–163
Cook, Tim, 62–63
Cooke, Rob, 33
corporate social responsibility (CSR), 93–94, 180
Cowell, Simon, 106
credentials, for learning, 153–154
C-Suite, leadership and, 10
cubicle farms, replacing, 172–174
Cultivate: The Power of Working Relationships (Barrett), 93
cultural issues
  gender and, 36–37
  relationships and, 92–93
  See also globalization; workplace culture
Cultural Transformations (Mattone), 50
curiosity, 147–150, 194
customers
  change and, 186, 187–188
  experience of, 121–122
  technology and demand of, 131–132

workplace culture and, 43–45
cybercrime, cost of, 123

D
Deep Blue (IBM), 125
Dell EMC, 36
Deloitte, 91–92, 145, 165, 166
demographics
  change needed for future-proof workplace, 2–3, 5–6
  in Europe, 103
  population shift in U.S., 102–103 (*See also* diversity and inclusion)
Derezin, Mike, 51, 71
design. *See* workspace design
development, of subordinates, 38
digitization
  big data, 122–124
  change needed for future-proof workplace, 2–3, 4–5
  See also technology
disruption. *See* change
diversity and inclusion, 101–117
  action needed for, 115
  bias issues, 107–110, 112–114
  change needed for future-proof workplace, 8–9, 15–16
  empathy and, 112
  future-proofing career with, 117
  future-proofing company with, 116
  initiating change for inclusion, 192–193
  in leadership roles, 103–105
  neuroscience issues of, 109–115
  overview, 101–102
  population shift in U.S., 102–103
  stereotyping and, 101–102, 105–106, 111
Donne, John, 77
Drucker, Peter, 12, 47

E
Economist, 18
Ellis, Greg, 67
e-mail, 127–129
emotional connections
  brain and unconscious bias, 111
  importance of, 9

human resources
  change and, 17, 187–188
  development of subordinates, 38
  employees and purpose, 71
  flexible workforce, 84, 131–134,
    166–167, 176–178
  jobs and, 4–5, 85–88, 149–150, 153
  learning and hiring practices, 158–161,
    163–165
  modernizing people and processes, 144
  performance management, 165–166
  providing learning opportunities for,
    155–156
  relationships and, 87
  technology and, 131–135, 137–139
  See also diversity and inclusion;
    learning; relationships; workplace
    culture

I
IBM, 11–12, 125, 140
"I" education, 150
Implicit Association Test (Harvard
  University), 116
Inc. magazine, 113
inclusion. *See* diversity and inclusion
Industrial Revolution(s), 84–85, 130, 143,
  195
innovation
  leadership and, 23–24
  workplace culture and, 51
inspiration, purpose and, 68–69
Internet
  digitization and freelance economy,
    130
  Internet of Things, 123
  social networking compared to
    networking, 94–96
iPhone 7 (Apple), 133

J
Japan, globalization and, 6
jobs
  automation of, 153
  career change, 149–150
  career lattice, 85–88
  digitization and change to, 4–5
  skills for (*See* learning)

  See also flexible workforce; human
    resources
journals, for learning, 169
Joy Inc. (Sheriden), 54
Jung, Carl, 109

K
Kaizen, 36
Keane, Margaret M., 72–73
Kellogg School of Management
  (Northwestern University), 10
Kelly Global Workforce Index 2013, 89
Khan Academy, 197
Kleinert, Jared, 70
"Knowledge, The" (British test for
  London Taxi drivers), 124
knowledge acquisition, 145–150
knowledge management, for learning,
  162–163
Kodak, 47, 64
Koushik, Srini, 140
Kouzes, Jim, 26
Kraemer, Harry, 10

L
leadership, 21–40
  change needed for future-proof
    workplace, 8–11
  "command and control" style of, 22–23
  consequences of, 26–27
  decision to lead, 37–38
  defining values for, 31–32
  developing, 161–162
  disruption and, 188–189
  diversity and inclusion in, 103–105
  future-proofing career with, 40
  future-proofing company with, 39
  greed and, 24–26
  leaders with heart, 32–37
  overview, 21–22
  personal values and company values
    for, 28–31
  privilege of, 28
  self-focused, 23–24
  for talent management, 158
  in twenty-first century, 27
  for workplace culture, 57–58
Leadership Challenge, The (Kouzes), 26